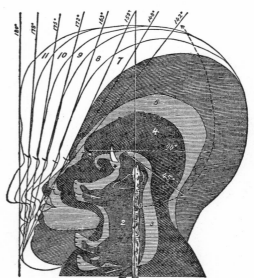

FIG. 1—THE SNAKE.   FIG. 6—BUSHMAN.
  " 2—DOG.   " 7—UNCULTIVATED.
  " 3—ELEPHANT.   " 8—IMPROVED.
  " 4—APE.   " 9—CIVILIZED.
  " 5—HUMAN IDIOT. " 10—ENLIGHTENED.
                        " 11—CAUCASIAN—HIGHEST TYPE.

PHRENOLOGY
FAD AND SCIENCE

A 19th-Century American Crusade

BY JOHN D. DAVIES

ARCHON BOOKS, 1971

ISBN: 0-208-00952-3
Library of Congress Catalog Card Number: 70-122405
Printed in the United States of America

This book is for Sara

Acknowledgments

My academic debts in connection with this enterprise are many and heavy. Professor Ralph H. Gabriel has unobtrusively directed not only the dissertation on which this essay is based but my whole approach to history; in the groves of academe I am proudly known as "a Gabriel student." The subject was unearthed in Professor George W. Pierson's seminar, and he has gone through several revisions of the manuscript with a fine eye and extraordinary care. Professors David M. Potter, Samuel F. Bemis, and James E. Roohan read an earlier version and made suggestions. Professor Robert E. Riegel looked over a synopsis of the material and suggested many fruitful leads for further research, based on his own profound knowledge of the contemporary sources. I have had interviews with Professors Edward Hungerford, John F. Fulton, Paul M. Gates, and Henry Guerlac, and with President A. Whitney Griswold, all of whom offered information and advice. Mrs. Edith Fox, Curator of the Collection of Regional History at Cornell University, kindly allowed me to consult the Fowler-Wells letters. The librarians of the Sterling Memorial Library and the Medical Library at Yale University, the New York Public Library, the New York University Library, and Smith College were unfailingly cooperative and sympathetic.

JOHN D. DAVIES

Smith College
February, 1955

Foreword

I hate this shallow Americanism which hopes to get rich by credit, to get knowledge by raps on midnight tables, to learn the economy of the mind by phrenology, or to acquire skill without study or mastery without apprenticeship. . . . Fourier and Miller and Dr. Buchanan will not heal us of our deep wound, any more than Spurzheim and the Flying Man, to whom they have succeeded.

Ralph Waldo Emerson

IN 1899 Alfred Russell Wallace, the eminent biologist, published a book called *The Wonderful Century,* which reviewed the progress of the past hundred years. After describing the great achievements of the 19th century in science and technology, he faced up to its failures, and the first (and worst) of these was the neglect of phrenology, "an example of the almost incredible narrowness and prejudice which prevailed among men of science at the very time they were making such splendid advances in other fields of thought and discovery." But if the adoption of this study had been slow, it was, he thought, inevitable: "In the coming century phrenology will assuredly attain general acceptance. It will prove itself to be the true science of mind. Its practical uses in education, in self-discipline, in the reformatory treatment of criminals, and in the remedial treatment of the insane, will give it one of the highest places in the hierarchy of the sciences." [1]

Despite Wallace's optimism, phrenology today, far from being accepted as a science, is considered a harmless quackery practiced upon the gullible at county fairs and the Coney Island boardwalk. What is more striking, it has faded from our memories as well as

1. Alfred R. Wallace, *The Wonderful Century* (New York, 1899), p. 193.

our beliefs: it is slipping away not merely from the present but from the past itself. In written American history it is recalled only as an obscure and amusing eccentricity of *The Sentimental Years* [2] and *The Stammering Century* [3] and *The Mad Forties*,[4] of interest only to the antiquarians of what Charles Beard called "the bathtub and bustle school" of social historians. The serious scholar tends to ignore phrenology as an amiable gaucherie of a prescientific age that knew not Freud: the standard social history of that generation devotes exactly one clause to the movement,[5] and the first page of the best chronicle of pre-Civil War reforms claims that "for too long have we paid amused attention to the fads and fancies of the early nineteenth century. Phrenology . . . and all the other eccentricities of the era have had more than their due share of the limelight. Alongside them were fundamentals of faith, crusades, reforms, and reformers whose effect on American civilization was profound and permanent." [6]

It is the thesis of this study that phrenology is deserving of detailed analysis, not "amused attention." That it is classified with alchemy and astrology today does not mean it was merely a fad, appealing only to eccentrics. No one denies that the science of one generation is the pseudoscience of the next: today the "science" of public-opinion polls has already been compared to phrenology,[7] and who can say what the reputation of Freud will be in the 21st century? In its own time phrenology, like Freudianism, was a serious, inductive discipline, accepted as such by many eminent scientists, doctors, and educators; its aberrations were the results not so much of charlatanism or credulity as of the limitations of early 19th-century scientific method and medical techniques. However

2. E. Douglas Branch, *The Sentimental Years, 1836–1860*, New York, 1934.

3. Gilbert Seldes, *The Stammering Century*, New York, 1927.

4. Grace Adams and Edward Hutter, *The Mad Forties*, New York, 1942.

5. Carl R. Fish, *The Rise of the Common Man, 1830–1850* (New York, 1927), p. 245.

6. Alice F. Tyler, *Freedom's Ferment* (Minneapolis, 1944), p. i.

7. "The election returns of Truman's election, of course, have made any detailed criticisms of the polls superfluous; the polls are now one with the 'science' of phrenology." A. J. Liebling, "The Wayward Press," *New Yorker*, 24 (Nov. 20, 1948), p. 71.

mistaken some of its anatomical deductions may have been, scientific it was in its determination to study the mind objectively, without metaphysical preconceptions. Its priority in this field is recognized in the histories of medicine and psychology, and many of its fundamentals are as commonplace today as they were radical a century ago.

Aside from its physiological and psychological significance, phrenology was an important cultural influence in America, especially in vitalizing many varieties of reform movements. Like Darwinism and Freudianism, it was one of several waves of European scientific thought which washed upon these shores and were dissolved into social philosophies and peculiarly American configurations. Although posterity has not been so charitable to Franz Gall's reputation as to Darwin's and Freud's, in the 1830's his discipline was probably better known than theirs have ever been—since in its vulgarized form it was more easily understood and of more immediate utility. Phrenology embraced a consistent system of thought, but it also encompassed a complex of ideas in many divergent areas of human behavior. The manifold deductions from phrenological principles were taken up by a variety of reformers to rationalize their crusades. Thus a large volume of literature was produced upon many topics, and through lecturers, societies, magazines, books, and periodical articles phrenological tenets were dinned into American ears until the appropriation of their peculiar vocabulary by fiction and popular speech made them familiar to everyone. The counterattack of conservatives and skeptics in general and the pulpit in particular added a certain gravity to the belief in this new "science" and made ignorance or indifference almost impossible; in some ways its acceptance was a shibboleth of liberalism. The smoke of the bitter public debate, as well as the genuine conflagration underneath, is worthy of serious study.

True, the advent of phrenology on the American scene was not a major event;[8] American history does not need to be revised in

8. What *is* "a major event" in American intellectual history? It might be noted that Transcendentalism, of which our literary historians make so much, receives about the same amount of space as phrenology in Merle Curti's *The Growth of American Thought*, New York, 1943.

the light of my findings. But as another John Davies discovered when he wrote *Microcosmos* (1570), there are advantages to concentrating on a single theme within a limited span of time.[9] Intellectual history needs not more intuitive interpretations of the grand sweep but "analysis, by historians, of both the process and the dynamics of intellectual change within a relatively short period of history. Thus we can see intellectual change at work and observe, as it were under a microscope, the complex of factors that promote it. From such a detailed experiment we can perhaps deduce general laws of intellectual change and its causation." [10]

In the modern era it is difficult to prove that any given philosophy—rationalism, democracy, romanticism—originated with a certain school and specifically influenced other thinkers to a given degree. Since the basic philosophic ideas have been current in some version or other for many hundreds of years, the critic can argue that the idea did not "move" but was ubiquitous, that instead of "influencing" its advocate, he simply seized upon it from the standard repertory to rationalize a course of action already decided upon. But phrenology, if it does nothing else, avoids this particular historiographical problem, for it is as close to an original idea as anything that ever existed, and for this reason the geographical and social momentum of its unprecedented concepts can be precisely measured. Although its novel theories tended to take on the protective coloration of the ideas with which they blended, we can trace the phrenological thread as it moves like a radioactive isotope through the thought tissue of the early 19th century.

For these reasons an examination of the American career of phrenology may be regarded as a sort of controlled experiment, a

9. Whitney R. Cross has said it well: "Microcosmic study has definite advantages. . . . In the small theater of investigation, integrated treatment of cultural, social, economic, political and ideological causations may be more satisfactory than in larger ones. . . . I have tried by the microcosmic approach to produce a reliable and broadly meaningful bit of general American history." *The Burned-over District; the Social and Intellectual History of Enthusiastic Religion in Western New York, 1800–1850* (Ithaca, 1950), pp. vii–viii.

10. Franklin L. Baumer, "Intellectual History and Its Problems," *Journal of Modern History, 21* (1949), 195.

case study in the movement and influence of ideas. How do they change in the transit from Europe to America? What are the vehicles of their dissemination? How does the process of "fractional distillation" operate, in which various parts of a complex of ideas break away and affiliate with existing knowledge at different levels? Is America congenial to pure science? These are a few of the questions which such an inquiry as this may help to answer.

The study falls into three parts: the first section, in five chapters, is a chronological narrative of the rise and spread of phrenology in America; the third section is a summary. The second division, an eight-chapter topical analysis of the impact of phrenology on various categories of social thought, may suggest something of the interrelation between the subdivisions which academic departments have staked out in our historical past, the connection, for example, between literature and physical anthropology and between architecture and religion. To quote Baumer again:

> the method best calculated to succeed, in my opinion, is the study of the different branches of thought in relation to each other. Comparative studies of this kind are few and far between. We have a plethora of general histories and monographs on special aspects of theology, philosophy, science, historiography, literature, economic and political thought. But where is the history that cuts across these disciplines and relates the one to the other? . . . What we need are detailed studies of the interrelationships of thought in relatively brief periods of time.[11]

For these several reasons a study of phrenology may be worthy of more than "amused attention."

11. *Ibid.*, pp. 193–4.

Contents

PART ONE. HISTORY

Chapter 1. A New Science Is Born

The intellectual outburst created by the doctrines of Gall and Spurzheim may be appropriately described with that which occurred after the discoveries of Galvani (1791) and Volta (1799). . . . New visions were entertained of vital forces and powers, and for a short time discussion and speculation knew no bounds. So it was with phrenology. It attracted immediately to its study many of the credulous but also some of the best intellects of the age. They formed themselves rapidly into societies for discussion of the new and suggestive hypotheses of the continental authors, and journals were soon established to commemorate the results of their deliberations.

John F. Fulton, 1927

PHRENOLOGY originated as an experimental science with the a priori assumption that mental phenomena have natural causes which can be determined. In modern terms it represented the union of a theory of localized brain functions with a primitive behavioristic psychology. Although it is remembered today only as a method of reading character from the contour of the skull, its true foundation was the theory that anatomical and physiological characteristics have a direct influence upon mental behavior. For purposes of classification the human race was divided into four basic psychological types: the "nervous," distinguished by a large brain, delicate health, and emaciation; the "bilious," marked by harsh features and firm muscles; the "sanguine," characterized by large lung capacity and moderate plumpness; and the "lymphatic," with rounded form and heavy countenance. These correspond roughly to Sheldon's three divisions of ectomorph, mezomorph, and endomorph, since the bilious and sanguine are obviously variants of the mezomorph; indeed, phrenologists refined the four original

types to three—the "mental," the "motive," and the "vital"—thus
anticipating Sheldon's system. As in his classification, these models
were not mutually exclusive but customarily mixed in varying proportions.[1]

The second cardinal belief of the new psychology was that the
mind is not unitary but is composed of independent and ascertain-
able faculties, some thirty-seven in number. These were elaborately
catalogued under such rubrics as, for example, Combativeness,

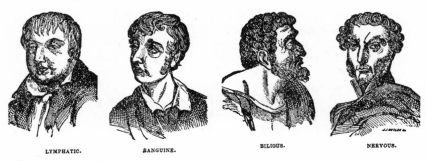

LYMPHATIC.   SANGUINE.   BILIOUS.   NERVOUS.

Character analysis: the phrenological "types"

Veneration, Benevolence, Adhesiveness, Amativeness, and Language. Third, the phrenologists believed that these aptitudes or
propensities are localized in different "organs" or regions of the
brain.

The final theorem was the most famous as well as the most controversial but does not necessarily follow from the first three: the
development of these thirty-seven organs affects the size and contour
of the cranium, so that a well-developed region of the head indicates
a correspondingly well-developed faculty (propensity) for that
region. Consequently, it was thought that a man could make a fairly
accurate character analysis by studying the shape of a subject's head
in conjunction with his temperament.

To this theory of brain structure the postulates of a behavioristic

1. "The new science of anthropometry was a descendant in the third generation from a discredited ancestral phrenology." William H. Sheldon, *The
Varieties of Human Physique* (New York, 1940), p. 12. For a contemporary
exposition of phrenological principles see below, Appendix.

psychology were added. According to the phrenological doctrine of the growth of the faculties through exercise, a person can consciously develop and cultivate his virtues, i.e. socially desirable propensities, and inhibit or atrophy his vices, i.e. over developed, socially undesirable propensities. From this a social philosophy was projected which appealed particularly to reformers: men are not born corrupted by original sin; they inherit varying sets of individual propensities which can be individually determined and scientifically altered. Man's mind and character were put into his own hands, and the potential role of education in social reform became apparent.

Phrenology was thus a popular system of psychology which professed to explain scientifically the riddle of the ages: how is man constituted? The greatest object of curiosity to any human is himself, the second is his neighbor—and to these problems phrenology proposed explanations which were simple and logical, if specious. As psychologists do today, phrenologists told their age how to be happy, how to choose a profession, how to select a wife, how to raise children; not only did they maintain that education was of supreme importance but they offered detailed curricula and pedagogical techniques. Other sociological and psychological applications were the diagnosis and cure of insanity, the conduct of penology, and the reform of the criminal. The human mind is directly affected by bodily health, according to phrenological theory; therefore such mundane topics as physical exercise, proper clothing, correct diet, and fresh air were legitimate objects of research and prescription by the mental therapist. Finally, for the common man, who did not understand philosophy, psychology, or physiology, phrenology afforded a "scientific" method of character analysis, aptitude testing, and vocational guidance. Thus this young, experimental, and somewhat protean science was of interest to scientists, doctors, social thinkers, and reformers of every description; and for those persuaded by its optimistic and utilitarian interpretation of life it offered hope for all and a vision of ultimate perfection.

This rather large pearl was built around a grain of sand in the form of the student speculations of a German physician named

Franz Joseph Gall, originator of the phrenological theory of brain structure if not of the optimistic philosophy later based upon it. Born at Tiefenbrum in Baden in 1758, he studied at Strasbourg and after 1781 at Vienna, where he took his M.D. in 1785 and soon

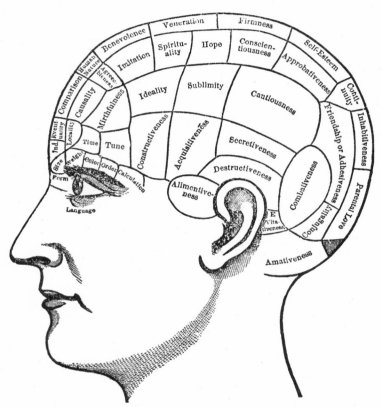

Thirty-seven faculties: the phrenological "organs"

enjoyed a large and fashionable practice; in the 1790's he was offered the position of Court physician but preferred to remain with his extensive private clientele.

It was at this period that he turned his attention to some conjectures of his student days. He had previously observed that his fellow pupils who had good memories all had prominent eyes, and from this he inferred an organ of verbal memory behind the eye-ball. After a great deal of tedious experiment and careful observation he evolved the theory of cerebral localization outlined above. While this doctrine was basically derived from the teachings of Lavater—that character and disposition may be judged from the features of the face and the form of the body—Lavater had meant simply that the features were expressive of the soul. But Gall reversed the premises of physiognomy in a peculiarly materialistic fashion: character and intellect, he maintained, were simply the sum of the combined functions of the organs of the brain. Character *was* the brain.

When the Austrian government in 1802 forbade as subversive of religion and morals the lectures on his novel concepts which he had been giving for the past five years, Gall left Vienna on a speaking tour, accompanied by his pupil and colleague Johann Gaspar Spurzheim (born near Treves in 1776), who became associated with Gall after attending his lectures in 1800. For five *Wanderjahre* Gall lectured in the towns and universities and courts of Germany, Switzerland, and the Low Countries. This campaign brought him sensational success among the medical profession and literati and afforded him opportunity for further observation, experiment, and refinement of his theories; he was internationally famous, not to mention notorious, when he took up residence in Paris in 1807 and commenced public lectures once more. The next year in collaboration with Spurzheim he submitted a memoir on his anatomical researches to the *Institut* of France, but because Napoleon had berated the scientists for learning their anatomy from a German, it was disapproved.

Francis I had invited Gall to return to Vienna but he preferred to remain in Paris, where he was physician to ten ambassadors, had a large practice, and was considered a savant. Soon appeared the first volume of his magnum opus, *Anatomie et physiologie du système nerveux en général, et du cerveau en particulier* (Paris, 1810–19), which ultimately comprised four large folios and an atlas of illustrations. Later he published a revised edition of the main body of his work, entitled *Sur les fonctions du cerveau et sur celles de chacune de ces parties*. Metternich thought his the greatest mind he had ever known, and at Gall's death in 1828 he was justly mourned as a pioneer scientist and honest investigator who had left some portions of his topographical charts of the human brain blank because he did not know what faculties resided therein. His fame still rests upon many new discoveries in cerebral physiology, as well as his new and controversial doctrine of human psychology.

Spurzheim collaborated with Gall on *Anatomie et physiologie du système nerveux,* although his name was omitted from the title pages of the last two volumes because he had departed for England. His mind was of a rather different type: in addition to exploiting his own talents as a scientist, he played Brill to Gall's Freud. His historic function was to popularize phrenology, and he began to publish under his own name and to change some of his mentor's concepts, a course which soon led to an estrangement between them. It was Spurzheim who coined the word phrenology, "science of mind"—which Gall refused to use—and who by changing one essential added to the science the role of a philosophical movement. Gall accepted the existence of evil in the world and particularly of evil propensities in mankind, even labeling one region of the brain "Murder." The great majority of men, he thought, were composed of mediocrities, and he emphasized the creative role of genius and its destined function to command; his science would be the instrument by which the elite could govern effectively and rationally the mass of mankind. In keeping with the aristocratic clientele with which he had been associated, his was neither a democratic nor a liberal creed.

Spurzheim, on the other hand, deliberately omitted from his categories all faculties which were inherently evil; on the contrary, all were intrinsically good and only from the abuse of them could evil result. Mankind was created potentially good, and in contrast to Gall's cynical pessimism, Spurzheim looked forward to the perfection of the race by the aid of phrenology. Although Gall had recognized the philosophical implications of his theories, in general he had adhered closely to the discipline of experimental psychology —he was, as Metternich described him, "a man of facts, who detested theories" [2]—but Spurzheim, to his mentor's intense dis-

2. *Phrenological Journal, 17* (1844), 155.

approval, wandered into metaphysics as well as speculation on education, penology, religion, and other nonanatomical concerns. In this new view science and religion merged; phrenology revealed the laws of nature which God had established, which it was man's duty as well as God's will to follow. "The great aim of all his inquiries into human nature, was to search out the will of God in the creation of man. Obedience to his laws he considered as the highest wisdom, and most expansive freedom." [3]

In addition to these new directions for phrenology, Spurzheim perceived new vistas and entered upon missionary activities to propagate the faith among the ignorant. After mastering English in six months, in 1814 he undertook a lecture tour in Great Britain. Phrenology was by no means unknown there at this time; as early as 1803 the *Edinburgh Review* could say, "Of Dr. Gall and his skulls who has not heard?" [4] But England was afflicted with xenophobia after the Napoleonic Wars and was suspicious of quackery. When Spurzheim opened his English campaign with a dissection of the brain before the London Medico-Chirurgical Society, the medical profession evinced interest in his demonstration of the fibrous nature of the brain; but no very great interest about phrenology as such was aroused, and a course of lectures attracted an audience of only forty, a tepid reception duplicated in Bath, Bristol, Cork, and Dublin.

Spurzheim published at this time an English version of his theories, entitled *The Physiognomical System of Drs. Gall and Spurzheim, Founded on an Anatomical and Physiological Examination of the Nervous System in General, and of the Brain in Particular, and Indicating the Dispositions and Manifestation of the Mind.* It was brought to the attention of the British public by a lengthy, vituperative notice in the *Edinburgh Review,* a journal at the time enjoying considerable authority in the scientific world. These two sentences are typical:

The writings of Drs. Gall and Spurzheim have not added *one* fact to the stock of our knowledge respecting either the *struc-*

3. Charles Follen, *Funeral Oration . . . of Gaspar Spurzheim* (Boston, 1832), p. 23.

4. Quoted in *Phrenological Journal, 4* (1826–27), 1.

ture or the *functions* of man; but consist of such a mixture of gross errors, extravagant absurdities, downright misstatements, and unmeaning quotations from scripture, as can leave no doubt, *we apprehend,* in the minds of honest and intelligent men as to the *real ignorance,* the *real hypocrisy,* and the real empiricism of the authors. . . . Such is the trash, the despicable trumpery, which two men, calling themselves scientific inquirers, have the impudence gravely to present to the physiologists of the nineteenth century, as specimens of reasoning and induction.[5]

Spurzheim hastened to Edinburgh to confront his adversaries on their own ground and for a demonstration dissected a brain with the offending pages of the *Edinburgh Review* open before him, taking up its objections point by point before the doctors and literati of the Scottish capital. After this successful retort to his accusers, he remained for seven months in Edinburgh and lectured once more in London before returning to Paris in 1817.

The sale of Gall's and Spurzheim's works, however, was inhibited by the pall cast by what was later referred to in phrenological history as "the Edinburgh reviewer." But among Spurzheim's auditors in Edinburgh was a brilliant young barrister named George Combe. Combe, who had been deeply troubled by the Calvinist training of his youth, eagerly seized upon this optimistic new science and commenced an intensive study of it. The result was total conversion and his decision to devote his life to writing and lecturing upon phrenology, and in its history his part yields precedence only to Gall's and Spurzheim's. Although he learned to dissect the brain according to the technique which Spurzheim had perfected, Combe had no medical training and his extensive writings were concerned solely with the technique of "cranioscopy" and the application of its principles to the reformation of human affairs. He and his brother, Dr. Andrew Combe, with other enthusiasts formed a phrenological society in Edinburgh, which had a large membership and an active life. In 1823 it published a 500-page volume of *Transactions,* consisting of the various papers read at its meetings, and

5. *Edinburgh Review,* 25 (1815), 250, 268.

instituted a quarterly *Phrenological Journal,* which was to have a distinguished career for the next twenty-four years.

The result of the activity of the Edinburgh and other phrenological societies and the writings of the two Combes was the granting of a more respectful hearing by the periodicals of Great Britain, both medical and literary, and when Spurzheim returned to London in 1825 his lectures were packed. By the 1830's phrenology had given rise to some sixty-six books and pamphlets which had run through many editions, and the young science was being nourished by twelve phrenological societies, which furnished readers, authors, and audiences for the many lecturers on the subject. One W. R. Henderson in 1832 bequeathed his sizeable estate to promulgate phrenology, and the trustees executed this commission by subsidizing large and cheap editions of *The Constitution of Man* (1828), the best known and most inspirational of George Combe's works.

As a science, then, phrenology seemed to have a bright future, since it had more general acceptance than had the geology or botany of the period, for example, and more devotees versed in its principles and terminology. But phrenology claimed to be more than an esoteric science—it represented itself as a social philosophy and popular movement as well. Great Britain, however, was the only country in which there was any organized interest outside the medical profession, and there the *Phrenological Journal* at times had as few as three hundred subscribers and was kept alive only by the devotion of a succession of editors scattered throughout the country. The societies were small and served no function beyond that of upper-class debating societies; in keeping with the aristocratic structure of British society, little thought was given to how phrenology could awaken general interest and achieve a popular base. This was a problem young America was ready to accept, and the solution it found was typical for its period.

Chapter 2. Transit of the Atlantic

The prevalence and popularity of phrenological views may seem to require explanation. It is well known to most of our readers, how suddenly the doctrine established itself, and how rapidly it gained ground in this region. No sooner had its late distinguished apostle appeared in our city, than a *pentecost* was witnessed, such as philosophy had not known before, since the days of the later Platonists. All tongues were loosed, and a strange onomastic was in every man's mouth. Heads of chalk, inscribed with mystic numbers, disfigured every mantelpiece. Converts multiplied on all sides, some converts of the Covenant, and some proselytes of the gate. A general inspection and registry of heads took place. In defiance of the apostolic injunction, hands were laid solemnly on all men, and many by such imposition were ordained teachers. A cast was given them as diploma, *"una cum potestate publice praelegendi"* . . . In short, this theory of man obtained a speedy and signal triumph and all the higher principles of our nature were in danger of being entombed in the little *tumuli* of the brain.

Boston Christian Examiner, 1834

IN EARLY 19th-century America there was little interest in or knowledge of phrenology. Previously the colonial frontier of British culture, the United States had recently sued for political divorce and was now attempting to add cultural independence to political isolation. Nevertheless, the world of ideas does not recognize artificial boundaries, and for all the hyperpatriotism of the Early National Period, much of the old cultural intercourse went on as before. Evidence of acquaintance with phrenology began to appear in the 1820's. The vehicles of dissemination were two—European books and Americans who had studied abroad.

Before 1820 references to it in the press were scattered and hostile. The *Analectic Magazine,* a sort of digest of foreign thought, presented a summary of the theory of phrenology, along with an indignant condemnation on religious grounds, "since it degrades the mind to a piece of mechanism [and] indirectly denies all moral government." [1] Probably the first American in phrenology, in time if hardly in influence, was Nicholas Biddle, the Philadelphia banker, who had attended Gall's lectures at Carlsruhe in 1806 and 1807 and ever after kept a skull which Gall had marked for him. But in the 1820's interest became more common, at least in medical circles. Dr. John C. Warren, Harvard's famous professor of medicine, in 1808 had commenced a study of Gall's works and had been an auditor of Spurzheim's lectures in 1821 at Paris; he incorporated this new discipline into his college lectures and beginning in 1820 made it the subject of an annual address to the Massachusetts Medical Society. In 1823 Professor John D. Wells of Bowdoin returned from Europe, where he had listened to Gall, and each year thereafter explained and recommended phrenology to embryonic doctors. Proof of medical attention is shown by the formation of the Central Phrenological Society in March, 1822, at Philadelphia —composed largely of doctors and headed by the eminent Dr. William Physick—an association which thereupon began an ambitious and embattled career. The new organization was supported by the *Philadelphia Journal of the Medical and Physical Sciences* as well as the *Select Medical Library,* both edited by the well-known Dr. John Bell, also an official of the society.

The leading American of the decade in evoking interest in this new science was the famous controversialist Dr. Charles Caldwell. On a trip to Europe in 1821 to assemble a library for Transylvania University's new medical department, of which he was the founder, he had attended Spurzheim's lectures in Paris. To his own classes he began lecturing in the same vein, converting 175 out of 200 he said, and then taking off on peripatetic tours through the West and venturing as far east as Boston, Baltimore, and Washington. In the latter two cities, as well as in Cincinnati, he was responsible for the formation of phrenological societies, and he soon acquired the sobriquet of "the American Spurzheim." In all his medical crusades Caldwell was a violent polemicist and combated abusively "the

1. *Analectic Magazine, 6* (1815), 64.

spirit of animosity and mischief roused against me . . . by all I have done . . . toward the promotion of the knowledge of phrenology." [2] In phrenological terminology, "his Destructiveness and Self-Esteem [were] very large," [3] which was a circumlocution for "pugnacious and conceited personality." "For many years he stood almost alone its able advocate, its ever ready champion and defender, who, for every blast of obloquy, ridicule, and sophistry, directed against the novel doctrines, had an overwhelming counterblast of nervous argument and withering truth." [4]

In the decade of the 1820's the great number of books being published in English on phrenology began to find their way across the Atlantic and were circulated throughout the educated classes as well as the medical profession. The works of George and Andrew Combe became popular and the more formidable writings of Gall and Spurzheim well known. An American edition of George Combe's *Essays* appeared in Philadelphia in 1822, together with a 150-page addition by the editor, Dr. John Bell, while Combe's *The Constitution of Man* (1828), the best known and most inspirational of all phrenological books, enjoyed something of a vogue, especially when the Swedenborgians republished it in Boston. Even native products began to appear when George H. Calvert, an unconventional member of the famous Baltimore family, wrote his own *Illustrations of Phrenology* (1832); the introduction was original, even though the succeeding articles were taken from the *Phrenological Journal*. Charles Caldwell wrote his *Elements of Phrenology* (1824), hailed by the *Phrenological Journal* not because of its scholarship but because it was the "first original publication on phrenology by an American author." [5]

As might be expected, works on such a new and radical subject

2. Charles Caldwell, *Autobiography* (Philadelphia, 1855), p. 303. He continued (pp. 303, 426): "never . . . have I been free from a contest against some opinions or doctrines which I consider erroneous. . . . for many years I labored as strenuously against violent opposition, and at first alone . . . for the first introduction, and the ultimate establishment of the science of phrenology."

3. *American Phrenological Journal*, 5 (1843), 380.

4. *Phrenological Journal*, 16 (1843), 127.

5. *Ibid.*, 2 (1824–25), 113.

met something of a mixed reception. William Ellery Channing reported to his friend Combe on *The Constitution of Man* that "a gentleman of Philadelphia bought 50 or 100 copies—all he could find—for distribution, believing that he could not do more good," [6] while Ralph Waldo Emerson called it "the best Sermon I have read for some time." [7] The *American Journal of Education* closed its review of *The Constitution of Man* "by recommending it to the whole community," [8] even if later the same year it reminded its readers "we are not among the *enthusiasts* of this newborn science." [9] The *Knickerbocker,* always hospitable to new ideas, hailed George Calvert's little volume as illustrating the principles of "a truth so obvious that it will soon be thought absurd to question it." [10] The *Southern Review* spoke in terms of measured and thoughtful disagreement in reviewing Combe's works when it gave honor to whom honor was due "for knowledge of the structure of the brain and the connection between the intellect and physical causes," yet found the details of phrenology "most distinctly absurd and untenable." [11] Most reviews were much harsher than this, since the native credulity of American journals was tempered by the novelty of this new doctrine, its foreign origin, and the habitual sarcasm with which British reviewers handled it. Soon phrenologists in the New World had developed that sensitivity and martyr complex which was one of the hallmarks of the new scientists both at home and abroad. As Dr. John Bell complained, phrenology was "the subject of serious argumentation, or playful allusion—at times, of pointed satire or coarse invective"; [12] his point being that the comments were almost invariably adverse. Dr. Alexander Coates grumbled in the same vein: "Nothing but root and branch work will please these critics. . . . Our pursuits are looked upon

6. Charles Gibbon, *The Life of George Combe* (2 vols. London, 1878), *1*, 221.

7. Ralph L. Rusk, ed., *The Letters of Ralph Waldo Emerson* (6 vols. New York, 1939), *1*, 291.

8. *American Journal of Education, 4* (1829), 300.

9. *Ibid.,* p. 541.

10. *Knickerbocker, 2* (1833), 319.

11. *Southern Review, 5* (1830), 278, 279.

12. *Philadelphia Medical Journal, 8* (1824), 172.

by many with so unfavourable an eye as almost to amount to a persecution." [13]

The event which produced a genuine popular enthusiasm transcending the basically medical and scientific interests of the 1820's was a tour by Spurzheim himself, to propagate his science, to study the nation, especially the Indians and the slaves, and (he said) to see William Ellery Channing. Landing in New York on August 4, 1832, an event significant enough for Philip Hone to note it in his diary, he made the decision to proceed at once to New England, since New York at that time was suffering from an epidemic of cholera. New York was then as now a cosmopolitan city, accustomed to a constant procession of foreign celebrities and curiosities, and if he had chosen to make there what proved to be his sole American appearance, he would perhaps have been remembered only as the peer of Fanny Wright, Fanny Elssler, or Charles Dickens.

Within a week Spurzheim was off to New Haven, where Yale College was holding its commencement exercises. The distinguished foreigner made quite an impression when he attended the ceremonies; Professor Benjamin Silliman, with whom he stayed, said "the Professors were in love with him" and "with only one exception, no stranger ever visited the United States who . . . possessed the power at once so fully to absorb and gratify the public mind." [14] The medical profession also derived "great satisfaction" from his public demonstration of brain dissection. He then continued on to Hartford, where he made memorable conducted tours of the Institution for the Deaf and Dumb, the Retreat for the Insane, and the State Prison.

By August 20 he was at his destination, Boston, and that month initiated at the Atheneum a series of eighteen public lectures, which later had to be transferred to the Masonic Temple because of the size of the crowds. This same course was simultaneously delivered in Cambridge for the benefit of Harvard College, as well as a lecture series on the anatomy of the brain for the Boston Medical Society. In addition to this strenuous schedule of shuttling back and forth

13. *Ibid.*, 7 (1823), 75, 79.
14. *American Journal of Science*, 23 (1833), 356.

between town and gown, he embarked upon an industrious round of civic functions, inspections of the local schools and prisons, the exercises of the Phi Beta Kappa Society, and, inevitably, Harvard's commencement. Dr. John Collins Warren showed him "all the attention due a scientific stranger," [15] and the hours left unoccupied were taken up by innumerable conferences with the interested, skeptical, or merely curious. Even after six weeks of this exhausting regimen he refused to abate his activity, so important did he judge the success of his mission, but in his last lecture he was observed to be laboring under a severe fever; his health broke, and the ministrations of Dr. James Jackson, Boston's illustrious surgeon, were not enough to save him from an untimely death on November 10.

The first citizens of "the Athens of America" concerted to give this internationally famous stranger an appropriate burial. Dr. John C. Warren preceded his public autopsy at Harvard with a lecture on his teachings, while James G. Audubon and other artists made sketches of the departed. As a medical memento Dr. William Grigg afterward kept in his office at the Atheneum the mighty brain of Spurzheim, which appropriately, as the *Boston Medical and Surgical Journal* pointed out, weighed fifty-seven ounces. The morning after his death the visitor's friends assembled at his apartment to make the funeral arrangements; the committee was headed by President Josiah Quincy of Harvard, aided by Nathaniel Bowditch, Harrison Gray Otis, Joseph Story, Joseph Tuckerman, and others, while John Pickering, Thomas W. Ward, Nahum Capen, and Bowditch took charge of his estate.

Under such auspices the funeral was a great event. While the bells of the city tolled for what was called "a public calamity," some 3,000 citizens made their way to the Old South Meeting House, and in their midst marched the Boston Medical Society in a body. Professor Charles Follen of Harvard made a lofty memorial oration, followed by an "Ode to Spurzheim," composed by the Reverend John Pierpont and sung by the Handel and Haydn Society, which concluded thus:

15. Edward Warren, *Life of John C. Warren* (2 vols. Boston, 1860), 2, 13.

> Nature's priest, how true and fervent
>   Was thy worship at her shrine!
> Friend of man,—of GOD the servant,
>   Advocate of truths divine,—
> Taught and charmed as by no other,
>   We have been, and hoped to be;
> But while waiting round thee, Brother,
>   For thy light—'tis dark with thee! [16]

He was the second person to be buried in Mount Auburn Cemetery, beneath a marble monument contributed by William Sturgis, a prominent merchant.

Thus ended Spurzheim's mission, though it is debatable whether he could have attracted more attention by continuing his living activities than by this spectacular demise. Boston was the center of the flowering of New England, and his "lectures excited great and lively interest; they attracted alike the fashionable and the learned, the gay and the grave, the aged and the young, the skeptic and the Christian. Our most eminent men, as well as humble citizens, were early at the Hall to secure eligible seats." [17] And these "most eminent" were worthy of note; as the *Boston Medical and Surgical Journal* took pains to point out: "Among the constant attendants on the course, are our most distinguished physicians, lawyers, and divines, and citizens best known for their scientific and literary attainments." [18] Nathaniel I. Bowditch commented in the same vein to his brother in Paris: "the course of lectures in Boston was attended by a more brilliant and select company than ever before listened here to any other lecturer upon any subject whatever." [19]

Upon this fabulous audience Spurzheim seems to have made the most striking impact, and that despite his thick accent and halting English. The *Boston Medical and Surgical Journal* mourned the

---

16. J. G. Spurzheim, *Phrenology in Connexion with the Study of Physiognomy*, ed. Nahum Capen (Boston, 1833), "Biography of the Author," p. 138.

17. *Ibid.*, pp. 107–8.

18. *Boston Medical and Surgical Journal*, 7 (1832), 162.

19. *Transactions of the Colonial Society of Massachusetts, 10* (1904–06), 80.

death of "a great and good man," [20] Benjamin Silliman remembered the "amiable, winning simplicity of his manners, and his unpretending good sense, and good feeling." [21] Park Benjamin, editor of the *New England Magazine,* spoke from personal acquaintance that "we would not exchange, for the highest favors of the goddess of fashion, one of the golden hours we have spent with this philosophical and benevolent man." [22] Sarah J. Hale in her *Ladies' Magazine and Literary Gazette* fondly recollected that "those only who have seen his face when suddenly kindling with the enthusiasm and benevolence, and the smile that broke over his features . . . can understand the expression of countenance that accompanied [his] words. . . . The effect on my own feelings will never be forgotten." [23] Another writer on the staff of the *New England Magazine,* even though he personally was opposed to phrenology, granted that "if a man ever lived who deserved the love of all men, it was he; for he was a perfect philanthropist. . . . Those obsequies, what a noble tribute to mental and moral greatness! A city (for the first time on this side the Atlantic) in mourning for a man, who had never fought a battle, or worn a badge of office." [24]

Spurzheim's lectures, his personality, and his dramatic decease together acted as a catalyst to produce a flare-up of American interest in phrenology, and it is the purpose of this study to analyze in successive chapters the interaction between phrenology and various aspects of the American scene in that generation. Here it is necessary to mention only that there was a spate of publicity as cheap and readily available editions of Gall, Spurzheim, the Combes, and others were published by American firms; references to them became common in the magazines and newspapers as they were advertised and read and reviewed, and many articles and books of native authorship appeared on phrenology and allied subjects. Lyceums and debating societies added the new doctrine to their

20. *Boston Medical and Surgical Journal,* 7 (1832), 225.
21. Follen, *Funeral Oration,* p. 16.
22. *New England Magazine,* 4 (1833), 43.
23. *Ladies' Magazine and Literary Gazette,* 5 (1832), 571.
24. *New England Magazine,* 5 (1833), 79.

agenda, as a sure guarantee of interest and controversy. Special magazines were published for its devotees, who banded together in societies with their own libraries and collections of skulls.

The *American Journal of the Medical Sciences* mourned, "the prophet is gone, but his mantle is upon us." [25] When the *London Medical Gazette* sardonically reported this event as caused by "brain fever," along with the cheerful hope, "we know not on whom, if on any, his mantle will descend; but we hope nobody will be foolish enough to bring it across the Atlantic," the *Boston Medical and Surgical Journal* retorted hotly that "we can assure the editor of the Gazette that a highly gifted individual has been found in the city *foolish* enough to assume the mantle of our departed friend." [26] The crown prince referred to was Dr. Jonathan Barber, a teacher of elocution at Harvard, who soon was lecturing around the towns of New England, bearing not only the mantle but Spurzheim's own collection of drawings and casts to illustrate his talks. Other auditors and exponents of Spurzheim became associated with Dr. Barber in spreading the new gospel, for example Dr. Dunkin, his son-in-law and also of Harvard, and William B. Fowle, teacher at the Boston Monitorial School. Once Dr. Barber ventured as far south as Charleston, South Carolina, and Savannah and Augusta, Georgia; but mainly the efforts of these three were confined to the New England area. In any case, they were restricted to "audiences of a most respectable character"; [27] for example, in April, 1833, Dr. Barber gave a course in New Haven to an audience which included many lawyers, nearly all the clergy and Yale faculty, and Benjamin Silliman, who gave a speech of thanks at the concluding lecture.

Perhaps the high-water mark in phrenology, at least among the upper classes of the United States, was reached in the years 1838–40, when George Combe, now the foremost phrenologist in the world, followed in his illustrious predecessor's footsteps with an American lecture tour, coming upon the invitation of some American philanthropists. Warned about Spurzheim's unhappy demise, he took

25. *American Journal of the Medical Sciences, 12* (1833), 473.
26. *Boston Medical and Surgical Journal, 8* (1833), 105.
27. *Annals of Phrenology, 1* (1833–34), 144.

precautions against the same exhausting regimen,[28] especially the relentless curiosity of the Americans, and lasted out some eighteen months of delivering 158 two-hour lectures in most of the major cities of the East but without venturing west of the Appalachians. In addition he gave morning classes on the principles of character analysis; although not a doctor, he demonstrated to the medical profession Spurzheim's technique of brain dissection and held conferences with thousands of interested individuals. His audiences were large, usually between 300 and 500, a number which increased when newspapers and magazines with a total circulation of some 25,000 reprinted seriatim the stenographic transcriptions of his New York lectures.

Following the example of his precursor, he initiated his tour in Boston. Despite the fact that only fifty handbills had been distributed in anticipation of his arrival—Combe visited cities only upon invitation, with a $750 guarantee—he in large measure duplicated Spurzheim's success with an average attendance of over 300. In New York City, the next stopover, Professor William M. Holland reported that "Mr. Combe is succeeding admirably. His first lecture was attended by five or six hundred." [29] His Philadelphia audience surpassed 500, and according to the *Eclectic Journal of Medicine* his lectures excited "continual interest." [30] At their conclusion he was requested to repeat the course immediately, which he did with an attendance of 350, and in the same manner made successful repeat performances in New York and Boston.

In addition to his talents as a publicist Combe was a brilliant Scotsman who moved with ease and poise in the best society. An intimate friend of William Ellery Channing, he enjoyed varying degrees of friendship with Samuel Gridley Howe, George Bancroft, George Ticknor, Nicholas Biddle, and many others, and made the

28. He was not exactly idle, however; his relative Fanny Kemble wrote that he had "parcelled out both his whereabouts and whatabouts, to the very inch and minute, for every day in the next two years to come." Frances A. Kemble, *Records of Later Life* (New York, 1882), p. 102.

29. Nahum Capen, *Reminiscences of Dr. Spurzheim and George Combe* (New York, 1881), p. 135.

30. *Eclectic Journal of Medicine*, 3 (1839), 273.

acquaintance of John Quincy Adams, Martin Van Buren, and
William Henry Harrison; he impressed Horace Mann so deeply
that the educator named a son after him. He was elected to the
American Philosophical Society and the National Academy of
Natural Sciences, while Rembrandt Peale did his portrait "for his
own gratification." With his wife, daughter to Mrs. Siddons and
cousin of Fanny Kemble, Combe was a personable advance guard
for phrenology and made many American friends. He was honest,
and a blunt and thoroughly British person who reported everything he saw with candid yet sympathetic eyes; while he thought
Tocqueville, lacking the proper phrenological spectacles, foresaw
entirely too pessimistic a future for the New World, he was glad to
return to Great Britain with all its faults. His three-volume *Notes
on the United States of North America during a Phrenological Visit
in 1838–39–40* (Edinburgh, 1841), revealing, entertaining, and yet
objective (despite the fact that all Combe's American earnings were
lost in the crash of his friend Biddle's Bank of the United States),
was promptly republished in Philadelphia and has become one of
the standard historical sources of the period; even Americans who
were mentioned in his conspectus, chronically sensitive from many
foreign scars, liked it, because "scientific knowledge and objects
gave dignity, interest and permanent value" to his work.[31]

Combe's audiences were large, but even more important was
the fact that they were from the intellectual elite of this country.
Sixteen two-hour disquisitions upon psychology were something
more than light entertainment, especially when the speaker possessed no particular "graces of elocution or fluency of speech," as
the *Eclectic Journal of Medicine* somewhat ungraciously pointed
out.[32] Combe claimed his Boston audience comprised the best set of
heads he had ever seen: "My eyes never rested on such a collection
of excellent brains . . . big headed, moral, intellectual and ener-

31. Henry T. Tuckerman, *America and Her Commentators* (New York,
1864), p. 221. The *Ladies' Companion, 15* (1841), 48, thought that his work was,
with the single exception of Tocqueville's, "the most sound and able exposition of America and her institutions, which has ever proceeded from the pen
of any foreign traveller."

32. *Eclectic Journal of Medicine, 3* (1839), 273.

getic Pilgrims, enlightened and civilized. Spurzheim's memory is warmly and delightfully cherished by them, and they were prepared for me in every way." [33] His auditors in Philadelphia "embraced professors, physicians, and men of the first grade," [34] in New York "the best hearers in the city." [35]

A typical example of his American tour was his sojourn in New Haven in February and March of 1840. His audience of 300, "for numbers and respectability, such as rarely falls to the lot of a public lecturer in this city," [36] "included most of the professors, and a portion of the students of Yale College, and a large number of the citizens . . . the largest class, in proportion to the population, which I have had in the United States." [37] Among the friends he made in this "most enlightened and agreeable society" were Denison Olmsted, Dr. Nathaniel W. Taylor, Noah Webster ("The Johnson of New Haven"), Jonathan Trumbull, General Dennis Kimberly, "and other highly accomplished men." [38] Between Combe and Professor Benjamin Silliman there already existed a warm friendship and mutual admiration. At the conclusion of the course ex-Governor Henry W. Edwards presented complimentary resolutions on behalf of the class, after which Silliman made a speech affirming the general truth and scientific validity of the new psychology—this was the fourth course on the subject for him. Since this was Combe's last lecture in America, the class purchased his collection of casts for the purpose of further study.

The sudden appearance of so much phrenological literature and the lectures of Spurzheim and Combe set off a sort of chain reaction in the intellectual world, and interest among this class reached its zenith in the 1830's. As Tocqueville observed, America has used the "principle of association" more successfully than any country in the world; members of the intelligentsia now banded to-

33. Gibbon, *Combe*, 2, 34.

34. Capen, *Reminiscences*, p. 6.

35. *Ibid.*, p. 135.

36. *New Haven Record*, March 21, 1840, as quoted in *American Phrenological Journal*, 2 (1839–40), 372.

37. George Combe, *Notes on the United States* (3 vols. Edinburgh, 1841), 3, 245.

38. *Ibid.*, pp. 245, 246.

gether in phrenological societies for the study and propagation of the subject in this institutionally minded age. These societies had their own club rooms, with libraries and periodicals and the indispensable collections of skulls, casts, and drawings. Regular meetings were held, at which the members presented papers on the principles of their science and its multifarious applications to human affairs. It was with these estimable gentlemen that George Combe had most of his contacts in the United States—they invited him here, made the arrangements for his lectures, secured the advance publicity, sold the subscriptions, squired him through their cities—and were responsible for most of the serious, legitimate interest in phrenology.

Between forty and fifty of these associations are known to have existed, but for illustrative purposes three examples will suffice. The first in America was the Central Phrenological Society, formed in Philadelphia in February, 1828. Dr. William Physick, the foremost medical figure of his generation, was its president, and among its long slate of officers the aforementioned Drs. John Bell and William Coates were the moving spirits; apparently to add that éclat without which no Philadelphia enterprise can succeed, a Biddle (Clement C.) was added as vice-president. At first the going was steep, confronted as the society was by public attitudes ranging from amused contempt to raucous jeering and by the unavailability of books and the lack of cranial casts. But the re-publication, at the instance of the society, of George Combe's *Essays* (with a special introduction by Dr. Bell) by the Philadelphia firm of Carey and Lea, the procurement of a large collection of skulls and casts from Edinburgh, the domestic manufacture of illustrative engravings and casts, and the inauguration of a series of public lectures resulted in a vigorous campaign against its detractors, the "forces of intolerance, the offspring of pride and indolence." [39] Proof of the interest and zeal which the Central Society had aroused, Dr. John Bell later claimed, was the size of George Combe's Philadelphia audience, his largest in the United States and exceeded by only one in Great Britain.

According to Charles Caldwell, another society was formed in

39. *Philadelphia Medical Journal, 4* (1822), 73.

Washington in 1824, the result of one of his proselytizing tours. Among its charter members were government officials, and in the usual fashion it held elaborate inquiries into skulls of more than passing interest; for example, its *Report on the Skull of Alexander Tardy* (Washington, 1828) analyzed the character of an executed murderer whose skull had been procured through the good offices of Dr. Alexander Brereton, Surgeon-General of the United States and secretary of the society. The most valorous episode in the association's history was its aggressive defense against Dr. Thomas Sewall of the local Columbian College, who delivered the most famous single attack upon the new doctrine (see below, pp. 140–2). The society demanded that he repeat his lectures against its favorite science for its benefit; when he refused by various circumlocutions to meet the membership in public debate, it published the correspondence, proving to its own satisfaction Dr. Sewall's bad faith and leaving him to the not so tender mercies of Dr. Caldwell.[40]

The career of the Boston society was representative, although the caliber of the membership was of course exceptionally high; it had the extraordinary inspiration of the founder himself and, so to speak, was the mother church: "Boston is the phrenological emporium on this side of the Atlantic—there Spurzheim labored, lived, and died, and to phrenologists the spot possesses peculiar attractions."[41] Professor Charles Follen spoke in his eulogy: "Let us take up the fallen standard from the hands of the dead,"[42] and that very night a committee met to draw up a constitution and by-laws. The society was incorporated by the Legislature, and its roster of 144 members, one-third from the medical profession and fifteen from the clergy, included some of the best-known Proper Bostonians, while the *Ladies' Magazine* hoped that feminine "couragement and approbation will aid in making the phrenological

---

40. *Proceedings of the Phrenological Society of Washington, Relative to the Two Lectures against the Science of Phrenology, Delivered at the Columbian College by Dr. Thomas Sewall, Professor of Anatomy and Physiology, in May, 1826,* Washington, 1826.

41. *Phrenological Magazine and New York Literary Review, 1* (1835), 48.

42. Follen, *Funeral Oration,* p. 28.

society . . . popular and permanent." [43] It carried forward a vigorous program of meetings and papers and programs—an outline of its activities for the year 1835 alone occupies five closely printed pages—as well as instituting a series of lectures for the public and promoting a magazine, *Annals of Phrenology* (see below, pp. 56–7). It purchased an extensive collection of casts, still preserved at the Harvard Medical School, which was basically that of Spurzheim augmented by numerous acquisitions from abroad; according to the society's catalogue, published in 1835, the exhibition included 416 items, with more than 100 "racial" skulls. Its members were responsible for promoting American editions of the works of Gall, Spurzheim, and the Combes, as well as publishing their own addresses and proceedings; the secretary, Nahum Capen, arranged for his own publishing firm, Marsh, Capen, and Lyon, to issue a whole series entitled *The Phrenological Library*. A prize of $100 was offered for the best essay *attacking* phrenology, a contest which found no takers. Once a year on the ritual occasion—the birthday of Spurzheim—the meeting was thrown open to the public, with organ music, prayers, benediction, and an annual address delivered by a prominent dignitary such as Dr. Samuel Gridley Howe, Dr. Elisha Bartlett, the Reverend John Pierpont, or George Combe.

In emulation of Boston and in response to the lectures of Spurzheim and his successors, a rash of phrenological societies sprang up throughout the country—amateur scientists banded together by the use of a particular jargon, that mild suggestion of persecution without which no in-group seems to acquire a sense of solidarity, the intrigue of the novel, and that appeal to utility which makes a missionary group function.

> I confess to considerable sympathy with the new association above noticed [the Baltimore Phrenological Society], for the very reason that will probably prejudice some others against it, and keep them from it, namely, its NOVELTY. Novelty, of itself, I confess, would be a poor recommendation for any movement; but I have such an utter dread of the STAND STILL

43. Quoted in *Phrenological Journal*, 8 (1832–34), 274.

system—"Conservatism," as it is commonly called—that any thing which proposes to keep the elements of society gently agitated, is pleasing to me. Nay, I would rather witness a very THUNDER STORM OF REFORM, occasionally, than the sickly stagnation which so generally prevails. It would act not unlike the electric storms that are common to our summers, purifying the social elements around us, and giving new vigor to the intellectual and moral manifestations of our lives.[44]

A catalogue of societies would include, on the fringes of the Bostonian universe, those of Nantucket, Worcester, Hanover, Providence, Hartford, Andover, Amherst, and Brunswick; the "Burned-over District" was as "enthusiastic" over this new religion as it was over them all, as evidenced by the Utica, Buffalo, and Oneida societies, in addition to those of the large cities of New York State. Most of the principal communities of the country had one, and there are references to many others in villages and towns throughout this nation and Canada.

Some of course lacked Boston's moral earnestness, not to mention the inspiration of Spurzheim's laying on of hands, and consequently did not enjoy such a long career. Mrs. Trollope acidly reported the Cincinnati society:

> Between twenty and thirty of the most erudite citizens decided upon forming a phrenological society. A meeting was called and fully attended; a respectable number of subscribers' names was registered, the payment of subscriptions being arranged for a future day. President, vice-president, treasurer, and secretary were chosen, and the first meeting dissolved with every appearance of energetic perseverance in scientific research. The second meeting brought together one-half of this learned body, and they enacted rules and laws, and passed resolutions, sufficient, it was said, to have filled three folios. A third day of meeting arrived, which was an important one, as on this occasion the subscriptions were to be paid. The treasurer came punctually, but found himself alone. With patient hope, he

44. The *National Era,* as quoted in the *American Phrenological Journal, 9* (1847), 290.

waited two hours for the wise men of the West, but he waited in vain: and so expired the Phrenological Society of Cincinnati.[45]

Harriet Martineau commented in the same sardonic vein; Spurzheim, she said, had made all America phrenology conscious, but "the light is always going out behind as fast as it blazes up round the steps of the lecturer. While Richmond and Charleston tear off caps and wigs and fair tresses are disheveled," other cities were forgetting what they had so rapidly become enthusiastic over. These transitory enthusiasms she attributed to the provincial character of America.[46]

Even if the mordant bias of Miss Martineau is discounted, she had hit upon a common criticism of the phrenological movement in America, as its partisans themselves admitted. After a time the societies each began to decline; as Nahum Capen recollected many years later about the slump of the Boston group, it was almost implicit in the nature of the cause: "after a time the subject ceased to be a novelty, and ceased to command special attention; as controversy tended to simmer down, new novelties began to take the center of the stage, while the eccentricities of the odder advocates of phrenology tended to identify the subject with themselves in the public eye." [47] Combe's visit represented a great step forward for the movement, but he himself was gravely disappointed, though far from regretting his trip. The audiences were not so large as he had been led to expect, and while the mental caliber of his followers was high, they did not seem to be the leaders of any mass movement: "a phalanx of very superior persons, most of them belonging to the learned professions, who are excellent phrenologists so far as the philosophy of mind is implied in the study . . . but they are theorists." [48] Although Combe and

45. Frances Trollope, *Domestic Manners of the Americans* (London, 1832), p. 94.
46. Harriet Martineau, *Retrospect of Western Travel* (New York, 1838), pp. 188–9.
47. Capen, *Reminiscences*, p. 124.
48. Combe, *Notes*, *1*, 126.

Spurzheim were talented publicists, their appeal was primarily intellectual and to the upper classes. Their audiences and the societies were made up, as another English commentator pointed out, of "*theoretical* phrenologists; phrenologists of the studio; usually men of liberal education, following the professions of medicine, law, or divinity, who study the subject in their leisure hours, and . . . advocate it principally by essays and discourses." [49] To quote Combe once more, "I was greatly misinformed as to the state of the *people's* interest in phrenology." [50] This failure of the phrenological societies to advance was typical of the whole movement at these social levels; to this point it seemed that America was duplicating the English experience—foreign lecturers arousing interest and local societies carrying it on through upper-class discussion groups—while the problem of projecting phrenological doctrine throughout the populace was ignored. But all this was before the brothers Fowler.

49. *Phrenological Journal, 16* (1843), 128.
50. Gibbon, *Combe,* 2, 77.

Chapter 3. Phrenology Made Practical

Permanent inequality of conditions leads men to confine themselves to the arrogant and sterile researches of abstract truths, whilst the social condition and institutions of democracy prepare them to seek the immediate and useful practical results of the sciences.

Alexis de Tocqueville

If a conviction of the truth and importance of the science of phrenology is ever to be forced home upon the minds of men, it will be, not so much by *reasoning* upon the subject, as by a *practical application of its principles.* What do the common people, or even scientific men, care about the *arguments* adduced in support of any new subject or science? Before they will believe in it, or even *listen* to it, they must see its truth *practically demonstrated.*

O. S. and L. N. Fowler, 1836

PHRENOLOGY thus far was modeled upon the British pattern and thus directed by and to the upper classes of society; to quote the prospectus for George Combe's Philadelphia lectures, "the members of the learned professions so-called, may be more particularly expected to take the lead in the business." [1] The British phrenologists, coming from an aristocratic society, were quite content that it should remain so. But America was in the midst of the age of Jackson, and the democratic ideology determined that the American experience with phrenology should be fundamentally different from its European counterpart. That the American phrenologists had different aims is shown by this diagnosis of Charles Caldwell: "In this republican country of ours we carry everything *by numbers*. It is here that *vox populi* is truly and practically *vox Dei;* and here every body reads, and not a few

1. Quoted in *Eclectic Journal of Medicine, 3* (1838–39), 34.

think. I have thoughts of endeavoring to avail myself of this state of things in behalf of phrenology." [2] For all his admirable intentions, Caldwell's method of diffusing the subject among *hoi polloi* was to write cheap and easily understandable works, but as we have seen, this did not seem to provide the key.

The American solution lay in quite another direction. English travelers conversant with the new psychology commented in chorus upon a new and particularly American phenomenon, for example:

> There is still another class of propagators of the doctrines, who have, in that country [the U.S.], done much in diffusing a knowledge of the subject,—with whose efforts in its behalf the faithful on this side of the Atlantic are less acquainted: I refer to the practical phrenologists; of whom it is characteristic that they give themselves altogether to the subject, and seldom have any other means of support than what they derive from their profession as phrenologists. These are a very numerous body in the States. [3]

In contrast to the amateur "phrenologist of the studio," the practical phrenologist in accord with the rising commercialism of the age exploited the new interest in things scientific—in other words, gave individual character readings at so much a head. Here lay the philosopher's stone that was to transmute theory to action. For practical phrenology purported to explain each man to himself— his virtues and vices, his potentialities, and limitations, how he could improve himself—as well as advise him on vocational guidance, aptitude testing, marriage counseling, and how to judge his fellows. These mundane questions, of course, Gall and Spurzheim and Combe regarded as beneath the level of their scientific inquiries and philosophical speculations; but the practical phrenologist would guarantee to solve these problems—for a price.

The first recorded example of this new profession appeared in 1833 at Amherst College, where in the backwash from Spurzheim's lectures phrenology had been designated the subject of a college debate, young Henry Ward Beecher being assigned the negative.

2. *Phrenological Journal, 4* (1826–27), 194.
3. *Ibid., 16* (1843), 128.

He wrote to Boston for literature and won the debate with a spectacular and crushing refutation of all its claims; but after the verdict he stepped dramatically down from the podium and announced his total conversion. Soon he and his classmate, Orson Squire Fowler, were lecturing on the science to the local Society of Natural History, while Fowler began to give character readings for his fellow students at the reasonable price of two cents *per caput*. This modest beginning was followed by speeches and demonstrations around the nearby towns of western Massachusetts by these typical college products, full of enthusiastic theories and reformatory zeal. At graduation Beecher decided to abide with his original call, although he remained a lifetime advocate of phrenology. He joined the (revived) Cincinnati society and used to harangue his long-suffering congregation on phrenology's benefits.

Orson Fowler had been studying for the ministry too and was waiting for the fall term of the Lane Theological Seminary to commence, but swayed perhaps by the forty dollars he and young Beecher had made on their previous tour, he heard a call from this new church. Initiating his younger brother, Lorenzo Niles Fowler, into the mysteries, he made a lecture circuit through upper New York State, his home region; when they met an enthusiastic reception in the Burned-over District, they moved upon the metropolises of New York, Philadelphia, Baltimore, Washington. Thus began their lifetime careers of writing, peripatetic lecturing, and giving examinations at so much per person.

Others of the same stamp, foot-loose young men, some educated but others not, took off on the lecture trail, and during the 1830's and 40's there was probably not a village in the nation that did not entertain at least one visit from an itinerant practical phrenologist. It was an unusual profession, often very lucrative, initiated in New England and dominated at first by New Englanders; in other words, this was a combination of the Yankee missionary and Yankee peddler, dispensing hortatory zeal to whoever would listen and useful wares to whoever would buy. The opportunities were so many and the field so extensive that not only were great numbers attracted to the new vocation, but in this house there were many mansions and some rather unusual practitioners. Even women became consultants, not just to their own sex either, since a Mrs. E. H. Sanford in 1849 was lecturing to "promiscuous" audiences, her lectures being "of a high moral order—pathetic and sublime." [4]

Not only were the speakers of a different caliber (and smaller bore) than Spurzheim, Combe, or their cohort, but there was a significant divergence in the content of the addresses themselves. The principles of the science were explained, it was true, if in a telescoped, vulgarized, dogmatic fashion, but most of the course was devoted to the application of phrenology to more interesting subjects, such as health, temperance, the raising of children, memory training, eugenics, matrimony, and religion. Even these lectures acted only as curtain-raiser to the performance proper to follow; to quote the handbill for the two Fowlers' course in New York City in October, 1836:

> The lecturers pledge themselves to demonstrate the truth of phrenology in any, and in every honourable way which the ingenuity of the incredulous may devise or propose. They throw out the challenge to disbelievers and opponents boldly, and without *condition or reservation*. They will meet opposition publicly, and on *any ground*—either by fair argument, or by application of the principles of the science to the heads and skulls of animals, or *to the heads of individuals selected by the audience*—either with or without *their eyes covered*—and let phrenology stand or fall by this test.[5]

This pragmatic sanction yielded high entertainment when the speaker offered his science to empirical proof, guaranteeing to analyze the characters of volunteers, none of whom he had seen before. Of course the cream of the jest was that these volunteers were familiar to the audience, and in an effort to deceive the visiting scientist the village idiot would be introduced or the county judge dressed in old clothes. If there were two lecturers, one would be sent from the hall and they would be forced to check separate diagnoses against each other. Or—the supreme test—the separate

4. Medina (Ohio) *Whig,* as quoted in *American Phrenological Journal, 11* (1849), 70.

5. Quoted in *American Phrenological Journal, 10* (1848), 511.

speakers would have to read heads blindfolded.[6] All this, of course, was a demonstration and inducement for the main source of income—private consultations on the following days for fixed fees, a sort of scientific fortune-telling or proto-psychoanalysis. A profitable vocation it was, too; at one time the Fowlers and Wells agency could list some twenty-six lecturers "in the field" as associated with them alone.

Their popularity was by no means limited only to the rural districts. These new types of demonstrations enjoyed a greater success in the large cities than Spurzheim or Combe ever did—if the size of the audience is taken as the sole criterion. A course of forty lectures in Boston in 1843 sometimes had audiences up to 3,000; well might the *American Phrenological Journal* say that "the city of Notions, has certainly a great *notion* for phrenology." [7] The differences between the performances and audiences of the 1830's and those of the 1840's may be gauged by the verdict of one of the few (apparently) who attended both: "with Spurzheim something was wanting to compel me to assent as fully. . . . Combe . . . omitted to give that satisfaction which is derived from an application of principles upon the spot where they are asserted. The Fowlers, with a courage amounting almost to rashness, have just dared to do what their great predecessors with greater caution had avoided." [8] In Philadelphia a congregation of 500 listened to twenty successive lectures; New York City had its own auditorium, Clinton Hall, devoted to phrenology and its ancillary sciences. As early as 1838 it was cited as one of the indices of civilization that in Honolulu, along with sidewalks and the customary scarcity of hard money, there were lectures on phrenology at the Seaman's Institute.

Nevertheless, practical phrenology was primarily a peripatetic vocation, devoted to exploring (and exploiting) the towns and villages and farms of an older America. Orson Fowler has left a description which epitomizes his methods and his audiences: "Let

6. This was no problem to a Dr. D. McMullen of Tennessee, who was blind! *American Phrenological Journal*, 22 (1855), 135.

7. *Ibid.*, 6 (1844), 23.

8. *Boston Daily Mail*, May 28, 1841, as quoted in *American Phrenological Journal*, 3 (1840–41), 430.

me plant a course of lectures in a little village, containing but a single tavern, two stores, and a blacksmith's shop, and a dozen houses, and they flock in from their mountains and their valleys for ten miles in all directions, and fill up any meeting-house that can be found. It is really astonishing, how much, not of interest merely, but of real *enthusiasm,* they evince, especially in reference to the *bearings* and *applications* of phrenology." [9] Here is another representative reaction, relatively sophisticated perhaps; from a student at Union College in the "Burned-over District":

> Last night attended a lecture on phrenology and today have had my cranium partially examined. Phrenology is fast rising to be a science & will no doubt ere long be studied as such. . . . The faculties the phrenologist made mention that I possessed were in almost all cases very true so far as I can judge of my own mind. I am rather inclined to think he neglects to tell the evil passion as in my case & many others none were noticed which I am confident we possessed. Perhaps interest promp[t]s him.[10]

Moving further west, this is the Illinois country of the 1840's, re-created by research as well as by the imagination of a novelist:

> The little man re-entered the tent and reappeared with a pointer, an armload of small clothbound books, and a cowbell, which he began to ring. A large crowd gathered. . . . "Why, friends, *why* are there so many blighted and unhappy lives? . . . Ladies and Gentlemen, I can answer that question. It is through a simple ignorance of the scientific principles that regulate human life. O, you say, Perfessor, don't go giving me any high-falutin' language about science because I can't understand it. Friends, it is my happy good fortune to have it within my power to open up to each and every one of you all the marvellous secrets of a great new science, by which you can achieve, like thousands before you, complete self-knowledge and self-control. . . .

9. *Ibid.,* 6 (1844), 23.

10. Manuscript diary of James McCall, Jan. 24, 1835, Collection of Regional History, Cornell University.

"I have myself become a specialist in the science of phrenology. I have examined the heads of three Presidents and many
other great and distinguished heads here and abroad, not excepting the crowned heads of Europe. By helping people to
become better acquainted with their strong and weak points, I
have been able to direct them to a fuller exercise or restraint of
certain faculties. Many hundreds and thousands of people have
already benefited from this instruction. Penniless paupers have
become the possessors of uncounted pelf. . . ."

Johnny sat for a while watching from the platform how the
people all rushed up and pulled dollars out of their pockets,
rudely grabbing for books in their haste. "—While they last!
While they last!" the Professor said. "One dollar, friends, while
they last! One hundred and fifty-four illustrations. Phrenological Self-Instructor. . . ."

Johnny walked away holding the little book in his hand. For
a few bright coins, dropped in a wooden cigar box, a future of
wonderful self-mastery had been opened up. In the presence
of the people he had become a child of prophecy; his consecra-
tion had been sanctified by the majestic adjective 'scientific' and
the formidable epithet 'phrenological.' Here, suddenly and by
accident on the Court House Square, there had been a confirmation of something Johnny Shawnessy had always secretly believed—that he was destined to be a great man and to find one
day the key to all knowledge. For a while, he felt jealous of all
the other people who had purchased the same cheap ticket to
intellectual beatitude, but when he saw the innocent, shy joy
on their faces, as they wandered somewhat confusedly like himself in the Court House Square, clutching their *Self-Instructors*,
he was thrilled to think that he was to be one of a whole community of Americans working together toward the creation
of a perfect republic.[11]

Finally, these are the Iowa pioneers of the next decade:

It was Indian summer, just before the school opened for the
winter, that our first phrenologist reached us and the use of the

11. Ross Lockridge, *Raintree County* (Boston, Houghton Mifflin Co., 1948),
pp. 74–5, 79, 80–1.

schoolhouse almost for a week was his. Of his science many of the prairie people never so much as heard. Representative of Fowler and Wells, with abundant pamphlets, books, and charts, a glib speaker, withal, *a minister soi-disant,* he would have preached to us on Sunday, forsooth, but his application came too late, to the disappointment, no doubt, of some.

Night after night, the house was full, first at ten cents and then at fifteen. Did not the mentor in our civic palace hold each day his solemn court, issuing, not without a consideration, charters in the name of O. S. Fowler, *duly signed;* drafts on the future for each lucky boy; life's highway stretching on visible, as usual, chiefly here and there on *heights only* . . . in many a manly heart ambition stirred; and doubtless beyond the meadows the noblest visions rose, even hovered above the handles of the plow. . . . Every one of them is going to be president of the United States, I reckon, one right after another, hand running.[12]

This institution was by no means a chicanery reserved by pitchmen for rustic yokels. To be phrenologized was a perfectly routine, even fashionable thing to do in that era. The reason for the fabulous circulation of the phrenological books, hundreds of thousands of copies of which were printed, was that most were given away with a phrenological examination and contained on the title-page blanks for the names of the examiner, the recipient, and the attainments of the latter in the various faculties. It was the Fowlers who had commenced this custom; back in Amherst days "the public demanded some record of their estimate of the size of the organs in the heads they examined, and the chart was produced first as a slip, then a sheet, afterward a pamphlet, and later a book of two hundred pages, and thus practical phrenology was begun and established." [13] Usually it was the Fowlers' books which were used, but some practitioners had their own charts printed, with appropriate endorsements, advertising matter, individual interpretations, and sometimes ingenious variations. For example, one John

12. Thomas Huston Macbride, *In Cabins and Sod-houses* (Iowa City, The State Historical Society of Iowa, 1928), pp. 42–4.
13. Nelson Sizer, *Forty Years in Phrenology* (New York, 1884), p. 15.

Fletcher, in his *Mirror of Nature,* had a day-by-day chart in which the recipient could grade himself in his exercise of his phrenological faculties in order to build up those in which he was deficient— a precursor perhaps of another foreign psychologist, Dr. Coué.

Now phrenology had a mass base and popular appeal, and many of the most prominent Americans felt that to have an examination was the conventional thing to do—to pay hard cash to learn "what they *are,* and what they *can* be, as well as how to make themselves what they should become." [14] One examiner, Nelson Sizer, alone made over 200,000 examinations. Advertisements for job applicants sometimes requested phrenological analyses along with references, while Horace Greeley quite seriously suggested that railroad trainmen be selected by the shape of their heads (below, p. 50). Among the examinations still preserved are those of James A. Garfield, Joseph Story, Nicholas P. Trist, John Brown, John Tyler, G. Stanley Hall, Elihu Burritt, Walt Whitman, and Chang and Eng. Joseph Smith's was published, Gideon Welles left his in his private papers, Robert Dale Owen included his in his autobiography, while Othniel C. Marsh and Roger S. Baldwin presented theirs to the Yale Library. These men were of course volunteers, who had paid to have the analyses made. On the other hand, virtually everyone in public life had submitted with more or less grace to having his cranial measurements taken as a concession to the curiosity of the public; the *American Monthly Magazine* featured in 1838 complete tables of the dimensions of the heads of "our great men."

Not least among the customers of the practical phrenologist was the mother anxious about her son or the worried youth in search of a profession, and such diverse personalities as "the cowboy detective" Charles Siringo, Clara Barton, the sculptor Clark Mills, and Bernard Baruch entered upon their varied careers at the advice of the specialist, although the prediction of another about Hiram Ulysses (later U. S.) Grant becoming President could hardly be classed as vocational guidance. Queen Victoria and Prince Albert had George Combe examine the heads of their large brood, and Senator Charles Sumner had him inspect his own battered cranium

14. *American Phrenological Journal, 8* (1846), 32.

after the famous beating by Preston Brooks. Benjamin Moran, Henry Adams' adversary in the London Embassy, wrote out phrenological analyses of his colleagues, as did Otto von Bismarck; Karl Marx always judged the mental qualities of a stranger from the shape of his head, as did Baudelaire, Balzac, and George Eliot. Henry George was accomplished enough to make an examination of himself. A random catalogue of 19th-century figures who accepted the rule-of-thumb aspect of phrenology could be expanded almost indefinitely.

This new approach and these new lecturers succeeded in reviving the phrenological societies, although in a different form and with new members. When Lorenzo Fowler lectured in Baltimore in 1846, the result was the formation of a society which met twice a week for more than nine months, but only by pursuing a wide range of topics. In 1847 Hartford brought forth a society with nearly 300 members meeting twice a week—but devoting one meeting to reform, the other to examining heads. Phoenix-like, the Washington association hit upon a new scheme to interest its members; every person was supposed to jot down the interesting heads seen during the week and expatiate upon them in meeting. The *American Phrenological Journal* explicitly warned the societies about the reasons for their demises: they consumed time by prosy essays, by being too speculative and not factual; for example, Philadelphia's "respectable society"—the use of the adjective is indicative—failed in 1839, while a later one whose object was to examine heads succeeded.

The British phrenologists had done everything possible to discourage this method of making converts to phrenology, since it induced belief without rational grounds for it; phrenologists should proselytize by study and explanation, by reason and not by faith. Furthermore, it was unscientific, even given the wide limits of phrenology. Illustrative of the way phrenology had gradually lost its original tentative and cautious nature was the fact that Gall himself had been rather dubious that character *could* be read from the shape of the skull: "I have never pretended to distinguish the influence, which modification of the forms of the cranium slightly marked, may have on the character, or how its corresponding

shades may be traced. My first observations have only been made
upon persons who were distinguished from other men, by some
eminent quality or faculty. I easily perceived that it was only
in such individuals, that I could find striking differences of
the head, and that I could distinguish well marked protuberances." [15]

Spurzheim was rather more optimistic about the new vistas for
the science but equally alert to their potentialities for charlatans;
he insisted that phrenology be studied only as a part of physiology
and "anxiously endeavored to prevent its becoming an instrument
of quackery and soothsaying, in the hands of the ignorant and pre-
sumptuous. He therefore constantly refused the requests of those
who wished him to point out their own characters, or those of
others." [16] R. H. Collyer, another British phrenologist lecturing in
the U.S. in the late 1830's "viewed with sorrow and indignation
. . . the self-styled phrenologists who were constantly springing
up in New York City, throughout that large state, and in fact, in
almost every city and town in the Union." [17]

The British phrenological publications, when they came to review the progress of the Americans, were torn between esprit de
corps and alarm. American phrenology had certainly surpassed the
English, had achieved a greater popularity than in the mother
country, but in so doing had also assumed a peculiarly American
configuration—but was it still phrenology? Were the practical
Americans simply popularizers or were they heretics? The British
verdict, in the main, was for the latter. The American in his public
performances was contravening all the principles of the science, not
to mention commercializing and vulgarizing them. He compounded base motives with unscientific procedure by omitting the
preliminary inquiries concerning age, health, and education "without which no phrenologist is competent to utter a philosophical
opinion," and the Glasgow *Phrenological Almanac and Psycholog-*

15. Quoted in Amariah Brigham, *An Inquiry concerning the Functions of
the Brain, the Spinal Cord, and the Nerves* (New York, 1840), pp. 129–30.
16. Follen, *Funeral Oration*, p. 23.
17. R. H. Collyer, *Lights and Shadows of American Life* (Boston, 1840), p.
15.

ical Annual appealed rhetorically that the new psychology be saved, in the words of the 92d Psalm, "from a Fowler's snare, and from the noisome pestilence." [18]

Consequently, the American phrenological societies of the 1830's, carrying on the high intellectual tradition in the British model, threw their weight against the rising tide of "practical manipulation." The Boston Phrenological Society, for example, said in its organ, the *Annals of Phrenology:* "it degrades the science not only, but gives rise to superficial converts . . . turns a dignified science into a system of legerdemain, and those who are really able to promote the true philosophy of man will be prevented from investigating the subject, on account of the repulsive appearance of the exterior. The rule should be, *examine no heads of living individuals of respectable standing.*" [19] Even in Boston, President Samuel Gridley Howe complained, the worst enemies were "those sophomores and blue stockings, who run about applying their callipers. . . . they do not take phrenology by the horns —they take it by the bumps." [20] George Combe commented in the same vein, when he noted the great number of practical phrenologists in the United States (several in Boston) "who examine heads and predicate characters for fees, and who are pretty extensively consulted. This practice, which, in the eyes of the uninitiated, resembles palmistry and fortune-telling, is said to have created a strong feeling of disgust against phrenology itself in the minds of men of science and education." [21] The *Southern Literary Messenger,* in reporting Combe's lectures in New York, made a like observation: "We acknowledge there is one stumbling block in the path of phrenology, which has hitherto obstructed its march to public favor, and that is the blundering ignorance and quackery of many of its professors . . . imposed upon the public by false representation of character deduced from a superficial view of the external organs; whereas the chief excellence of the science consists

18. Quoted in *American Phrenological Journal,* 5 (1843), 135.

19. *Annals of Phrenology,* 2 (1835–36), 131.

20. Samuel Gridley Howe, *Address to the Boston Phrenological Society* (Boston, 1836), p. 8.

21. Combe, *Notes, 1,* 126.

in its beautiful classification of mental phenomena, surpassing in that respect all the metaphysical systems of preceding ages." [22] Dr. Charles Caldwell, addressing the New Orleans Lyceum, struck the common chord: "quackery seems to be on the alert, and is profiting by the credulity of the ignorant," [23] while the *Phrenological Magazine and New York Literary Review* compared the practical phrenologists to "bankrupt rope-dancers [who should] forbear examining heads by the crown, (we mean silver) . . . and set yourself down in the solitude of study; become a true, judicious, and sincere phrenologist." [24] In his appendix to the published edition of Combe's American lectures, Dr. Alexander Boardman, secretary of the New York Phrenological Society, spoke out against the usual target: "It makes the enlightened phrenologist grieve over the abuse and degradation of his science, and gives countenance to the false and baneful impression that phrenology is akin to juggling and palmistry"; [25] while this diagnosis could be of service in the treatment of criminals, its uncertainties except in extreme cases were too great for an exact science.

Fowler's defense against this condemnation was that his was the only method by which the new science could be domesticated in America:

> And nothing is better calculated to make or confirm converts to phrenology than successful predictions of character, by a stranger. It is this which has driven, and is this moment driving, phrenology forward with a velocity and force absolutely irresistible. Let practical phrenology be encouraged; for it has done a work in this country which nothing else could have achieved; and by establishing, and popularizing and generalizing phrenology, it has laid the foundation on which those glorious superstructures of reform now so rife—now sweeping into oblivion the evils that enthral society, and placing man upon the true basis of nature—are based.[26]

22. *Southern Literary Messenger, 5,* (1838), 394.

23. *Phrenological Journal, 10* (1836–37), 247.

24. *Phrenological Magazine and New York Literary Review, 1* (1835), 23.

25. Alexander Boardman, ed., *Lectures of George Combe* (New York, 1841), p. 391.

26. *American Phrenological Journal, 6* (1844), 22.

Fowler was in an odd position vis-à-vis his English critics, since phrenology was supposed to be an international church maintaining a united front against the philistines, and furthermore he reprinted and marketed American editions of their works. The result was a sort of smoldering fratricidal feud, occasionally flaring into print; for example, English phrenology, according to him, was "rather too anxious on a *scientific* and *philosophical* basis, to the neglect of *practical* examinations. Mere theorizing and abstract reasoning, will never advance the interests of phrenology. . . . I fear the influence of this philosophizing spirit." [27] One representative of the American practical faction, Professor Mariano Cubi I Soler, arrived in France and wrote back to the *American Phrenological Journal* that phrenology was practically dead there, because no one but doctors and scientists were interested in it and experimenting with it, and then only as a means to understanding the structure and functioning of the brain!

What the theoretical phrenologists were objecting to, of course, was that the movement was rapidly dividing into two separate streams—the science of Gall and Spurzheim, and its technological application to character reading. If superficially it seemed that phrenology was advancing in public favor and publicity, actually it was this lesser branch that was expanding and threatening to devour its parent, which was quiescent. To the extent that phrenology was becoming popularized and vulgarized, it was losing its scientific character in the eyes of the intelligentsia. The educated classes were becoming alienated, while its friends were obliged to defend these unwanted "practical" allies, and its ubiquitous enemies were provided with a powerful weapon with which to assail it. To the public a phrenologist was a phrenologist, and when George Combe lectured in Hartford, a Mr. Young was covering the entire field in only two evenings with the aid of a "magic lantern," and another was explaining the whole science in one lecture at no charge— except for private consultations. Combe wrote wistfully from there that "in this city of 30,000 . . . Mr. [J. Stanley] Grimes and Mr. [Silas] Deane are regarded as far more distinguished phrenologists than I." [28] Scientific phrenologists were caught between two mill-

27. *Ibid., 4* (1842), 270.
28. Gibbon, *Combe, 2,* 79.

stones: "It becomes us as zealous advocates of phrenology, to become also guardians to the public for the purity of the science, by the bold exposure of quackery in all its forms. Much as the science has suffered from these misled philosophical opponents, it seems now likely to be travestied by a set of impudent and illiterate quack manipulators." [29]

Combe's fear that the practical phrenologist would lower the art to the level of palmistry and fortunetelling was a considerable understatement. In 1839 a brother phrenologist introduced himself to Combe in Boston:

> Originally he kept a store, and while in this employment became a little acquainted with phrenology. He examined the heads of his customers; his interest increased and then began to study it in books. He afterwards gave up the store, and commenced as lecturer, head-examiner, and magnetizer. He gives three lectures; the first free, at which he examines heads to excite interest. He charges 12½ cents (6½d.) to every person who attends each of the subsequent lectures, and he examines heads privately for fees. In all his lectures he gives the audience *facts*. "If," said he, "you were to address them with reason, you would never see them after the first lecture." Out of a village of 1500 inhabitants he generally drew from two to three hundred dollars in a week. He was a pure specimen of a Yankee. . . . I expressed my fears that his mode of proceeding did injury to phrenology in public estimation as a science. He said that he believed it did so with the better educated classes, but that the people would not receive it in any other way.[30]

In such a new and lucrative field there were almost too many opportunities. The columns of the *American Phrenological Journal,* itself the bible of practical phrenology and hardly the apostle of pure science, were filled with alarms against the impostors and charlatans attracted to the new vocation. One exhibited a giant and a dwarf as an added attraction, another assumed the name Combe, some entertained with song recitals; others were advertised on po-

29. *Edinburgh Psychological Annual,* quoted in *Magnet, 1* (1843), 24.
30. Combe, *Notes, 3,* 155–6.

lice handbills for falsely soliciting subscriptions as well as for conventional crimes. Still others pursued their profession in barrooms and took their fees in trade, and at least one added gambling to his ostensible calling. One itinerant bore the imposing title "His Royal Highness Prince Luximon Ray, M.D." and dispensed the *Grand Hindoo Poetical Chart;* [31] one can only wonder what his costume must have been. Some claimed falsely the sponsorship of Fowlers and Wells, while one was jailed for introducing himself as Lorenzo Niles Fowler. This last inspired the *American Phrenological Journal* to a blast against "Drunken phrenologists . . . vile and vicious vagabonds." [32]

Various devices were advertised, such as special hats and secret lotions to develop different organs of the brain, all of which hardly raised the science in the estimation of the discerning public. Incidents such as these, maintained Nelson Sizer, one of the most famous practitioners, "made our noble subject, in the minds of not a few, a hissing and a by-word." [33] This melancholy fact, of course, spoiled the pitch for all; Combe was unable to muster a lecture series in Baltimore, Cincinnati, or Providence, despite the prestige of his sponsors, because the populace had become completely suspicious of charlatanism. Perhaps an all too typical specimen of the calling was Huck Finn's friend, the Duke of Bridgewater, who advertised himself as "The celebrated Dr. Armand de Montalban of Paris who would lecture on the Science of Phrenology at ten cents admission, and furnish charts of character at twenty-five cents apiece."

31. (Cincinnati, 1854), 23 pp.
32. *American Phrenological Journal, 31* (1860), 42.
33. *Forty Years in Phrenology* (New York, 1884), p. 226.

Chapter 4. The Phrenological Fowlers

Those enterprising, philanthropical, phrenological publishers, Messrs. Fowlers & Wells, of Nassau street, are bringing out a popular series of books, chiefly relating to the natural sciences, which cannot be too highly recommended or widely circulated. They publish no work that has not a good moral aim and influence, and their imprint has become a guarantee to the public that the work which bears it is worthy of perusal. We rejoice to add that Messrs. Fowlers & Wells have been eminently successful as business men; and, in addition to the sure reward of the philanthropist, they are also rapidly accumulating a worldly fortune.

New York Mirror, 1848

Its [*American Phrenological Journal's*] present desire is this—to PHRE-NOLOGIZE OUR NATION, for thereby it will REFORM THE WORLD. No evil exists in society but it sternly yet calmly rebukes, and points out a more excellent way. No reform, no proposed good, but it strenuously enforces. It is the very "Head and Front" of that new and happy order of things now so rapidly superseding the old misery-inflicting institutions of society. In proof of this, see every article, every page of every number.

American Phrenological Journal, 1849

THE CHIEF figure in American phrenology during the 1840's and thereafter was destined to be Orson Squire Fowler, self-styled "great gun of phrenology in America." He did not exactly grasp the torch from the fingers of the departing George Combe; Fowler's flambeau was instead a unique product, the result of a kind of spontaneous combustion. So unexpected and displeasing was his success that Combe never bothered to call upon him, merely noting the American's presence and activities with a single sentence in Combe's account of his own travels, although he made a special trip to Louisville to meet what he conceived to be the leading phrenological figure in the New World, Dr. Charles Caldwell, and took pains to make the acquaintance of the first editor of the *American Phrenological Journal* and compliment him on the intellectual character of his editorial policy.

However great the contrast between Fowler and his eminent predecessors, the line of apostolic descent was direct, and in a consistent direction: from the scientist Gall to Spurzheim (who added missionary talents to his mentor's mastery of anatomy) to Combe (who was a zealot and a publicist and only incidentally a scientist) to Fowler (a thwarted evangelist who had only the crudest notions of medicine).

When the Fowler brothers arrived in New York City from Amherst in 1835 on their first lecture tour, they set up an office at 135 Nassau Street which gradually expanded into a combination lecture booking bureau, publishing house, and phrenological museum where character readings were given for fixed fees. Business became so brisk that they sent for their sister Charlotte, who developed into a practical phrenologist as well as a teacher of note, being known in phrenological history as the Mother of Phrenology. Lorenzo's wife Lydia also became a practical phrenologist and was well known as a lecturer and teacher when she entered the Central Medical College, where in 1850 she acquired the second medical degree awarded to a woman in the United States and was later appointed to the first medical professorship held by a woman. In 1843 a medical student named Samuel R. Wells joined the firm as an assistant, and when he married Charlotte the next year, he was taken into the concern as a partner and the name was changed to Fowlers and Wells.

The Fowlers were the first practical phrenologists; it was therefore appropriate that they should become the foremost. Their promotional schemes were an important reason for their success. At the beginning they had designed a chart which was given away with examinations; now this was increased to sixty pages, with the examinee's name, that of the examiner, and the date being written on the flyleaf, and individual notations of the various faculties within. For this form of examination the Fowlers charged one dollar (including the book); for a lengthy handwritten analysis the tariff was commensurately larger: three dollars.

One of the functions of the firm was to operate the famous Phrenological Cabinet, one of the showplaces of New York, with its thousands of skulls, casts, skeletons, exotic artifacts, and paintings, including Rembrandt Peale's portrait of George Combe. There

Salesman extraordinary: Lorenzo N. Fowler

the crowds of New York came to gawk and by the hundreds of thousands paid hard cash to learn their characters and potentialities; even a visit in person was not absolutely necessary: for the sum of four dollars Fowlers and Wells could even read character by mail, "from a good daguerreotype, the ¾ pose preferred." Since from the time of Yorick skulls have afforded food for thought, the Phrenological Cabinet was an exceedingly popular tourist sight, and although the ever present examiners and stenographers hovered deferentially in the background, admission was always free. This emporium displayed several thousand cranial reproductions of the noted, living and dead, appropriately contrasted with thousands of animals and variegated exotic savages as well as infamous murderers and pirates. Well might the editor of the *South*

Impresario and high priest: Orson S. Fowler

Carolinian say, apropos of his last visit to Manhattan, "ordinary citizens may find curious food for reflection, as well as the scholar or man of science. . . . We advise a visit to the establishment."[1] At the spectacle another enthusiast's lyre tuned forth:

> Such are the thoughts that crowd upon the brain
> And flash like lightning in the summer rain
> In this Museum of the human race—
> This grand bazaar of human head and face
> Peopled with busts and pictures of the past,
> With those who live, and those who live too fast. . . .

1. Quoted in *American Phrenological Journal, 28* (1858), 48.

Within the bonds of this metropolis
There is no museum so grand as this;
And yet the doors are opened widely, *free*
For all to come from every land and sea.
It is a link in the world's history.
We see with our own eyes the dome of thought,
Where genius wove the strains our souls have caught;
We touch the very skull where murderer planned
Reddened with human blood a human hand.[2]

Each year many thousands of New Yorkers and out-of-towners passed through the diagnostic services of the Phrenological Cabinet. So popular did it become that it occurred to employers here and there that the practical utilization of this science could be of value to others besides the individual concerned. Advertisements began to appear in the newspapers, such as this from the *New York Sun:*

AN APPRENTICE WANTED.—A stout boy not over 15 years of age, of German or Scotch parents, to learn a good but difficult trade. N.B.—it will be necessary to bring a recommendation to his abilities from Messrs. Fowlers and Wells, Phrenologists, Nassau Street. Apply corner of West and Franklin Streets.[3]

Horace Greeley was early converted to phrenology and reprinted George Combe's lectures in toto in his *New Yorker.* Now he suggested in his *Tribune* that trainmen be selected by the shapes of their heads in order to avoid accidents: "such men can be obtained; perhaps not at the lowest market price, but at prices somewhat equivalent to their required capacities, and nominal, the value of life, limb and property considered. But how? *By the aid of phrenology,* and not otherwise."[4]

With the Phrenological Cabinet becoming more and more popular, in 1851 Fowlers and Wells decided to open a branch office in Boston at 142 Washington Street, with one of their own

2. *Ibid., 32* (1860), 64.
3. Quoted in *ibid., 9* (1847), 19.
4. Quoted in *ibid., 15* (1852), 42.

associates, David P. Butler, in charge. Two years later this was followed by a Philadelphia establishment at 231 Arch Street, under the management of Nelson Sizer, who had already almost twenty years experience in lecturing and "manipulations" behind him.

Although the "retail" activities of Fowlers and Wells were lucrative indeed, its horizons by no means stopped there. Since the "reading" of heads was a recognized and far-reaching profession, the firm also engaged in the wholesale side by supplying the ubiquitous lecturers with paraphernalia of the trade. To lecture on phrenology or to study it seriously required equipment of a rather bizarre nature. Books on phrenology were easily come by, since all the large publishers issued them—especially those by British authors, there being no international copyright, and consequently no royalties—while charts could be readily printed to order. Still, the imprimatur of Fowlers and Wells seemed to the public a guarantee of reliability on these articles and by implication on the examiner himself.

The exhibits and illustrations, however, could be acquired nowhere else. A set of forty choice plaster casts was priced at twenty-five dollars and ran the gamut from John Quincy Adams, Voltaire, Sir Walter Scott, and Senator Thomas Hart Benton ("conscientiousness and mirthfulness not sufficiently developed") to the lower depths with Aaron Burr ("secretiveness and destructiveness very large") and a select assortment of depravity; scattered through the spectrum and illustrative of various attributes were the crania of Sylvester Graham, Napoleon, Elihu Burritt, and Henry Clay. For those with an appetite for realism human skulls "imported from ancient battlefields" were more expensive, five to ten dollars apiece, while those "of rare races" cost over thirty dollars, "animal skulls" less than a dollar. Paintings, drawings, and engravings of the brain and its structure were a necessity, but the *pièce de resistance* was a demountable model of the brain costing upward of twenty dollars.

By the 1840's a lecturer's versatility verged upon omniscience, and he branched out into related fields, especially physiology. For illustrations he could also turn to Fowlers and Wells—life-size anatomical drawings in color on rollers ($25 for a set of eleven),

wired and hung skeletons, oil paintings of "The Greek Slave,"
illustrations of deformed women (from tight lacing), or obstetric
plates. The omnivorous interests and promotional talents of Fowlers and Wells soon broadened the range of its items to include
galvanic machines (for self treatment), breast pumps, hand mills
for grinding cereal, and self-acting gates; and eventually they led
to the establishment of a special patent division to assist inventors.

These ingenious entrepreneurs were thus the suppliers of the
traveling phrenologists. But an allied opportunity arose, offering
kudos and financial return: who was to train them? In the beginning the firm used to accept apprentices, so to speak, though none
for less than a year because it did not want "smatterers." In 1842
Orson began giving short courses, at the Cabinet during the regular year, at his great home at Fishkill during the summer, to individuals or small groups before they began their journeyman training. These trainees were a source of revenue as well as future customers and served to carry forth the fame of Fowlers and Wells as
the central agency.

The suggestion was made repeatedly by the scattered and embattled devotees of phrenology that the new science should insti-
tutionalize itself in the same manner as other American reforms,
particularly should hold a convention, "since conventions are the
order of the day." Such a gathering, it was pointed out, would serve
three purposes: to establish a national phrenological society to
unite the scattered local associations; to found a phrenological
college which would award diplomas and thus ward off the mountebanks; finally, to codify the science and to settle the regrettable dis-
agreements and acrimonious schisms. The result was that in May,
1849, the suggested convention was called, and after a solid week
of sermonizing and open house at Clinton Hall, the national society was formed. Yet its membership was widely scattered and its
proper work never prosecuted with real vigor, everything requir-
ing time and effort being left to the Phrenological Cabinet in New
York and its managers.

As a result, a national association in a really vigorous form was
not born, and certainly neither authority nor agreement was
thrown against the new "discoveries" by various "scientific come-

outers" (surveyed below, pp. 131 ff.). But the Phrenological College was founded at the first meeting of the executive board of the national society in September, 1849, when the officers of the new institution of learning were chosen. The professors, to no one's surprise, were Lorenzo Niles Fowler and Nelson Sizer. In other words, Fowlers and Wells kept on running their Institute of Instruction, but now with the imprimatur of the American Phrenological Society.

Several years later some members of the American Phrenological Society, still dissatisfied with ignorant quacks who were defaming the name of science, petitioned the New York Legislature to incorporate the American Institute of Phrenology "for the purpose of promoting instruction in all departments of learning connected therewith, and for collecting and preserving Crania, Casts, Busts, and other representatives of the different Races, Tribes, and Families of men." [5] In the act of incorporation were listed as members of the governing body the names of Horace Greeley and Amos Dean. Each year a class was graduated—after a nine-months' course with a faculty of eight, mostly named Fowler—and in the first twenty years over 300 students, some from as far afield as New Zealand and Europe, received their diplomas and subscribed to the *Journal*. As one enthusiastic alumnus wrote in, "the fact of my having a diploma from the Institute at once raised me fifty per cent in the estimation of the best people of every place where I lectured." [6]

Another function of the firm was to publish books for the profession—not only to phrenologize America, but to Americanize phrenology, to adapt and domesticate the science to American tastes and national ideals. For this reason it was not enough simply to reprint the sacred originals from the European font. Between his extensive lecture tours Orson found time to write, and—as did all the Fowlers—he began to publish "that literal rush of ideas which now oppress my mind." In 1843 a British observer wryly commented: "in the literature of the science . . . Mr. Fowler has, of late years, taken a somewhat conspicuous place among the phre-

5. Sizer, *Forty Years in Phrenology*, p. 349.
6. *American Phrenological Journal, 80* (1885), 74.

nologists of America." [7] He had an instinct for making things popular by lowering the cost: "the principle of making everything cheap has always been a favorite with me, and has been a cardinal guide in all my prices." [8] Beyond that important consideration he had an instinctive rapport with the mind of the common man and a positive genius for the type of subject which would interest it, usually on the sensational side. His first book was entitled *Phrenology, Proved, Illustrated, and Applied* (1837), and it went through some sixty-two editions in the next twenty years; as has been indicated, the last word in the title is the key one. This was rapidly followed by *Love and Parentage* and *Amativeness,* both of which reached forty editions each of at least 1,000 copies; *Matrimony, Hereditary Descent,* and *Maternity* each sold over 50,000. Subsequent titles were *Self-culture and Perfection of Character, Religion Natural and Revealed, Education and Self-improvement, Temperance and Tight-lacing, Physiology Animal and Mental,* and *Memory and Intellectual Improvement,* concluding with a 900-pager in 1870, *Sexual Science.* His literary style is best characterized by the preface to the London edition of *Fowler on Matrimony:*

> Not content merely to expound and develop principles, and apply them to the predication of individual character, he sets himself the reformation of what is noxious in the fashions and institutions of his native land . . . temperance, education, and now Matrimony. He is, in a word, a phrenological Reformer; one may take exception to the *judiciousness* of his remarks, but cannot doubt his devotion and effectiveness. American by birth, constitution, character, and aspirations, it is not surprising that the style of his writings should be, as they have been called, "intensely American." He carries the "go-a-head" principle of his country into this as well as other channels, and is comparatively heedless of the *form,* so as he gets the *matter* expressed. . . . this "high-pressure principle" sometimes causes a slip of the pen. [9]

7. *Phrenological Journal, 16* (1843), 133.
8. *American Phrenological Journal, 5* (1843), 285.
9. Quoted in *ibid., 6* (1844), 111–12.

Orson was by no means the only one of the family who added literary endeavor to lecturing and examinations. All the Fowlers wrote, in fact, with the exception of Mrs. Orson Fowler, who apparently took little interest in the business. The best known of their several efforts were *Marriage: Its History and Ceremonies,* by Lorenzo Niles Fowler, and *Familiar Lessons on Phrenology for the Use of Children in Schools and Families,* by his wife.

In addition to the Fowlers' own works, the house also published those of Gall, Spurzheim, the two Combes, Dr. Charles Caldwell, and a whole galaxy of British and American phrenologists, as well as the *Phrenological Almanac,* which by 1848 was selling over 20,-000 copies a year. Always hospitable to new reforms, the firm took up the "water cure" and soon published dozens of volumes on its various applications, internal and external; in 1848 Joel Shew's *Water Cure Journal,* which had been floundering for three years, became part of the Fowlers and Wells empire, and its peculiar brand of journalism put it back on its feet.

Allied with this was an energetic receptivity to any unconventionality with moral overtones, and the Fowlers and Wells imprint became a sort of Haldemann-Julius of its day, with hundreds of inexpensive manuals on such topics as temperance, tobacco, physiology, obedience in women, vegetarianism, mesmerism, and the female anatomy. Beyond these were items of a more general (and neutral) character, on agriculture, horticulture, architecture, and etiquette, as well as assorted works from the pens of Walt Whitman, Andrew Jackson Davis, Robert Dale Owen, and Ralph Waldo Emerson. Another instrument of world reform—at least so it appeared to the enthusiastic Fowlers—was to be shorthand, and so they published, in addition to many books on the subject, a periodical devoted to it, the *Universal Phonographer,* appropriately printed in shorthand characters. Other Fowlers and Wells periodicals were the *Student,* a general miscellany "for the family and the classroom," and beginning in 1855 a weekly newspaper called *Life Illustrated,* a lively and successful journal patterned after its popular English contemporary, *Chambers' Journal.*

Between their extensive and variegated book lists and their periodicals, Fowlers and Wells claimed to have the largest mail-order business of any firm in New York City. While the prices were low—the policy being "the CASH principle, in order that we may deal on the CHEAP principle"—apparently the profits were considerable; from lecturing, examinations, writing, and publishing Orson claimed by 1842 to have made almost $75,000; and in the 1850's, as we shall see, he built a very large (and naturally enough, very unconventional) home at Fishkill which was later sold for $150,000.

One of the most pressing desires of those interested in the new science in this country was to establish a magazine like the Edinburgh *Phrenological Journal* or those of the other American reform movements, which would focus the interest and develop the *esprit de corps* of the embattled devotees scattered throughout the country, carry forth the battle on a national front rather than a series of local actions, announce strategy and gains, serve as a clearing house for new information and evaluate new literature, discern and denounce in a field with indistinct boundaries, and point with pride to or view with alarm the wandering comets which erupted from time to time into the new constellation. So anxious to effect this was the Washington Phrenological Society that it proposed in 1829 to publish an American edition of the *Phrenological Journal* of Edinburgh in order to popularize the subject on a national basis. This project, however, never came off.

As might be expected, Boston was first in this field of endeavor too. In 1833 the Boston Phrenological Society issued a prospectus for a quarterly, the *Annals of Phrenology,* to be published by the house of Marsh, Capen, and Lyon and edited by four officials of the society, including Nahum Capen and Nathaniel B. Shurtleff, later a famous Massachusetts antiquarian. Its first volume consisted of only two numbers, issued January and September, 1834, while the second appeared quarterly as advertised; both reached the stout proportions of five hundred pages and consisted of papers read before the Boston Phrenological Society, contributions from prominent American phrenologists retorting to newspaper attacks, news of the various societies and lecturers scattered about the country, and articles reprinted from the *Phrenological Journal* and the journal of the Phrenological Society of Paris. It was an estimable publication, edited with taste and commended by the *Phrenological Journal;* but it had a small circulation (about 300) and expired after two years.

Except for the *Phrenological Magazine and New York Literary Review,* a modest periodical issued in 1835 by the Utica Phrenological Society which never got beyond Volume *1,* No. 1, no further attempts were made until 1837, when the ubiquitous Fowlers initiated the *American Phrenological Journal,* a thirty-two page monthly. Orson distrusted his own editorial abilities—one of his rare exhibitions of modesty—and induced the Reverend J. A. Warne of Philadelphia to edit it for a consideration of $1,000, and the respectable firm of A. Waldie to act as proprietors for $500; as Waldie commented, "the prognostics of even its friends were sufficient to deter any person actuated merely by the expectation of making money, from embarking on it." [10] Nevertheless some 30,000 copies of an enthusiastic prospectus were distributed, and the magazine started off with 1500 subscribers. An admirable publication it was, spending $1,000 for authors' contributions in its first year, modeled carefully after the Edinburgh *Journal* and the *Annals of Phrenology.* After the first year the Reverend Warne was succeeded as editor by Nathan Allen, a medical student; George Combe condescended to call on Allen in Philadelphia and commented in his *Notes on the United States* that he was "a man of talent, industry, and high moral character, and he has impressed these qualities on his work." [11] Writing to the *American Phrenological Journal* from Boston, Combe added that he took pleasure in seeing "so much talent, zeal, and knowledge devoted to the cause." [12] In its introductory statement this publication declared explicitly that "we are not the advocates of unprincipled sciolists, who traverse the country, through its length and breadth, as practical phrenologists." [13]

So bright did the future appear and so thick was the backlog of articles and news that in the middle of Volume *1* the size was

10. *Waldie's Journal of Belles Lettres,* Pt. 2, No. 22 (Nov. 27, 1838), 1.
11. Combe, *Notes,* 2, 237.
12. *American Phrenological Journal,* *1* (1838–39), 96.
13. *Ibid.,* p. 7.

abruptly increased from thirty-two to forty-eight pages, with no advance in price. But even though several numbers of Volume 2 were sent gratis to the original subscribers, most of them failed to renew, and as the circulation dwindled, so did the deficits mount. Volume 3 closed with only 400 paying subscribers, not enough for the editor's salary, and the *Journal* was sustained only by Orson Fowler pouring into its dwindling coffers the not inconsiderable sums he was making from his tours. Once more America had failed to sustain scientific phrenology.

Prophetically enough, the last article in what appeared to be the last issue was a plea by Orson Fowler in defense of practical phrenology. Against the advice of his brother and the urgings of his wife (but encouraged by his sister Charlotte), Orson single-handedly took over the magazine, and it is indicative of the frenetic energy of the man that he not only earned by a strenuous schedule of lectures and examinations enough money to pay off its old debts and keep it going but also wrote virtually the whole magazine himself. The next four years were strenuous and critical ones for the periodical and for Fowler; "lecturing, examining, writing, running after paper, following up printer and binder, and called hither and yon perpetually," [14] he nevertheless some-how managed to get the *Journal* out to a declining list. Added to these embarrassments were the persecution by creditors, the bank-ruptcy of his printers, and the seizure of his stereotype plates for the debts of a friend. These next volumes were done in haste, urgency, and "in the singular number," with only the assistance of Charlotte; sometimes three numbers would appear at once; on one occasion three months were omitted "to make the volume numbers coincide with the end of the year." Occasionally Orson, unable to pay for articles by others, would simply bind in chapters from his forthcoming book (there was always a forthcoming Fowler book) and submit that to his readers, together with liberal reprints from the Edinburgh *Journal*. The last-named took haughty no-tice of this and denied Fowler's magazine the title of "Journal" because it simply reprinted books serially. Another change oc-

14. *Ibid.*, 7 (1845), 405.

curred in 1844, when in accordance with the proprietor's ideas of how to gain popular support, the price per year was cut from two dollars to one; at first the page count was reduced by the same ratio but later it was restored to its customary forty-eight pages.

America had refused to embrace scientific phrenology on any popular basis and now failed to sustain a periodical conducted on "philosophical" principles. Just as the focus of the science had shifted from the societies of the 1830's to the examiners of the 1840's, so did the editorial policy of the *Journal* slide to the other end of the spectrum, in accordance with the well-known opinions of the editor; "most of the subscribers and also the notices of it," Orson Fowler boasted, "speak of it as more practical and useful than former volumes." [15] Practical phrenology, then, had taken over the *American Phrenological Journal,* popularizing and vulgarizing its contents, with a concomitant loss of intellectual character and scientific integrity.

Now that the *Journal* was tailored to their own tastes and those of their audiences, the itinerant phrenologists rallied in this hour of crisis to save their magazine from imminent demise. Nelson Sizer, at that time touring the upper valleys of Connecticut, felt that "the *American Phrenological Journal* was the organ of a great cause, and the office and cabinet of its publishers, the Fowlers, must be regarded as the headquarters of phrenology in America, and that, whatever I could do to aid and strengthen headquarters, would be in the right direction for promoting the cause, and, of course, indirectly advancing my own interest. . . . We instantly wrote back: 'The *Journal* must not stop. We will be responsible for one hundred subscribers for next year.' I have his reply, saying: 'Your encouraging letter has decided the fate of the *Journal* for another year.' " [16] The lecturers, realizing the impending loss to the spread of phrenology in America, constituted themselves circulation agents and at every lecture would solicit subscriptions. A Dr. Ashbough secured forty-one subscriptions as a result of a single lecture in Cedarville, Ohio: "he is making phre-

15. *Ibid., 4* (1842), 316.
16. Sizer, *Forty Years in Phrenology,* p. 181.

nologists by the thousand and will certainly . . . procure hundreds of new names for the Journal." [17] Other subscriptions flowed in, 105 from the Connecticut Valley, forty from Mississippi, twenty-four from the Wisconsin Phalanx, twenty from lower Michigan. Other friends of "science" rallied round with cash contributions; C. Townson, a practical phrenologist of Ann Arbor, Michigan, wrote: "I can assure you that, *next to my religion,* I considered phrenology dearer to me than anything this side of heaven. It is my idol. . . . I shall send you $10 in a few days." [18] Others, similarly inspired, contributed in the same vein, $50 from Danville, Kentucky, $20 from Richmond, Virginia, $15 from Yazoo City, $50 from Erwinton, S.C., to mention only a few. Among the peripatetic lecturers the names of Buell and Sizer (who was later hired to run the Philadelphia branch) led all the rest, since they had guaranteed one hundred subscriptions and actually obtained three hundred. Their efforts were properly acknowledged by the *Journal,* in a typical example of its glowing prose:

> But Messrs. Buell and Sizer . . . are our most *efficient* agents. Every few days they send us a long list of subscribers, always accompanied with the *needful,* and what is more, they seem to enter, heart and soul, into the *reforming* spirit of phrenology, and into the views of the *Journal.* Gentlemen, we thank you; phrenologists should thank you, and those who, in after years, may read the *Journal* with pleasure and profit, should thank you for that efficient support. . . . Go on, brethren. Your reward is the very *doing* of this benevolent act.[19]

The rising circulation graph reached 1200 in 1843; this figure was doubled the next year, reached 5200 in 1845, 12,000 by 1846, and by the end of 1847, 20,000, one of the largest monthly circulations in the country. A geographic analysis of the circulation is significant, since it reveals that phrenology's growth was largely in rural areas and presumably among the less educated classes; it was not only moving downward socially, its direction of movement was

17. *American Phrenological Journal, 8* (1846), 125.
18. *Ibid., 4* (1842), 240.
19. *Ibid.,* p. 318.

outward, to the rural backwaters of the eastern states or to the frontier. Its most striking successes in Massachusetts were in "Lancaster . . . Chelmsford, Littleton, Westford, Groton, Fitchburg, Leominster, etc. . . . Why is it that in most of these old towns of the state, where public interest seems almost dead, and the individual member to think of scarcely aught but his land, his oxen, or merchandise, that so many converts should be gained to that science which was once considered unworthy of the public notice." [20] In 1844 Massachusetts and New York had the greatest numbers of subscribers, from the class just described, while the largest interest per capita was in Connecticut. But Ohio, which in 1844 had only 368 readers, climbed to 872 the next year and over 1,000 in 1846. By 1848 Ohio had a greater circulation per capita than any other state, followed by Wisconsin, with Illinois coming up fast. The *Journal's* explanation of why westerners should be interested in these new doctrines is reminiscent of Frederick Jackson Turner's: "They are pioneers in all reforms. They are composed of the most energetic and enterprising of all the older states. Hence their readiness to receive and promulgate phrenological science." [21] Another symptom of the venturesome mind of the West was the offer in 1837 of the chair of Mental and Moral Philosophy by the new University of Michigan to George Combe.

With the great increase in circulation and the formation of the partnership with Samuel R. Wells, as one issue informed the reader, "the pecuniary embarrassments of the editor are rapidly lessening." [22] The *Journal* now had money available to pay other writers and assistants to take on part of the administrative and editorial load, while Orson had the opportunity "to re-write, revise, re-arrange, compare, con over, and fully mature ideas." [23] But the character of the magazine changed not at all and was still a far cry from the *Annals of Phrenology* or the Edinburgh *Journal*, differing from them in the same ratio as Orson Fowler's lectures

20. *Ibid.*, 7 (1845), 344.
21. *Ibid.*, 10 (1848), 318.
22. *Ibid.*, 6 (1844), 168.
23. *Ibid.*, 7 (1845), 406.

from George Combe's. Its full title was the *American Phrenological Journal and Miscellany,* and in these years it seemed that the last word was the key one, with articles on shorthand, summer fruits, the orang-utang, tobacco and (other) slow poisons, and a monthly analysis (phrenological, of course, like that of the orang-utang) of a well-known contemporary, like Louis Kossuth.

Even this appeal to the popular taste was not enough for the editor, who planned to raise the circulation above the 30,000 mark. A new maneuver was inaugurated in 1851, when the *Journal* went from octavo to folio size but remained at $1 a year. "In this day of speed and progress . . . there seems to be a demand for a racy administration of science as well as literature"; [24] therefore the periodical was to take on a more attractive newspaper dress, use even more latitude in its choice of subjects, and popularize science "by giving to it the expansive freedom of the Spirit of the Nineteenth Century." In the new format one-half of the magazine was to be made up of departments of home education, agriculture and the mechanic arts, "general intelligence" (news), "natural science," a literary department, "and that which is adapted to the million," [25] all aptly illustrated with engravings. The rest, twelve pages, was to be devoted to the customary phrenology and physiology, and scattered throughout the whole another new feature—commercial advertisements.

With this arrangement the circulation curve continued to climb, even though large portions of the magazine were devoted to summaries of foreign and domestic news and articles on the locomotive, magnetic telegraph, and methods of horticulture. The readership grew to 35,000, 40,000, even 50,000, necessitating power presses and copper-faced electrotype. The *New York Tribune* and *New York Post* were among the constant advertisers in the *Journal,* just as their editors, Horace Greeley and William Cullen Bryant, were constant devotees of the science.

All this outpouring of books and their widespread diffusion, the mounting circulation of the *Journal,* and the aura of big business with which the Fowlers surrounded their subject aroused

24. *Ibid., 13* (1850), 1.
25. *Ibid.*

varying emotions in the guardians of the older scientific tradition. The spate of printed matter, either written by the Fowlers or inspired by them, was obviously a great contrast and an unwelcome one to the original version of phrenology. When *Phrenology Proved, Illustrated, and Applied* by the brothers Fowler was first received in England, it was cryptically reviewed by the Edinburgh *Journal:* "if it were English, it would unhesitatingly be set down as the work of empirics of some talent and more pretension," [26] containing numerous errors in its analysis of cranial structure. The first three volumes of the American *Journal* had been favorably received, but with the advent of Editor Fowler the wind shifted: these new volumes were "intensely *American* in their style, and entirely upon the Yankee go-a-head principle." Among these American characteristics were

> many inaccuracies . . . coincidences taken for causations . . . hasty generalizations are assumed as established laws, and much that is at present only guess-work, however shrewd, in the higher fields of phrenological speculation, are at once, sang froid, laid down as most established and determinate doctrine. . . . many announcements of the most startling nature . . . as cannot but . . . excite the risible faculties of even the most confirmed disciples of phrenology.[27]

Fowler reviewed the Edinburgh *Journal* in precisely the same spirit, but of course with the values, like a photographic negative, exactly reversed; he found it "intensely *English* in its character—philosophical, rather than practical; able, learned, profound, but less illustrative, and highly *orthodox*." [28] On another occasion he opined that English phrenology was "rather too anxious to place phrenology on a *scientific* and *philosophical* basis, to the neglect of *practical* examinations. Mere theorizing and abstract reasoning will never advance the interest of phrenology." [29]

Strangely enough, not all British representatives joined in this

26. *Phrenological Journal, 12* (1839), 96.
27. *Phrenological Almanac* (Glasgow), *2* (1843), 31–2.
28. *American Phrenological Journal, 5* (1843), 288.
29. *Ibid., 4* (1842), 270.

well-deserved condemnation of the Fowlers and their colleagues. Andrew Leighton, a member of the Liverpool Society, on a visit to the United States in 1842 made their acquaintance and ventured to justify them and their trade to his countrymen. Conceding their mistakes but defending their sincerity and integrity, he pointed out that many thousands annually visited Fowlers and Wells, among them some distinguished Americans, and many, struck by the verisimilitude of the diagnoses, were led to the study of the science. Furthermore, the practical phrenologists brought their message to every state of the Union, and since lectures always accompanied their demonstrations, sometimes the results were justified. George Combe, of all people, gloomily conceded the same point, that in America many intelligent devotees' interest had first been aroused by the demonstration of a practical phrenologist; and the fact that its doctrines could continue amidst all the abuses was a demonstration of the rectitude of its principles.

In other words, if the end justifies the means, the practical phrenologists were right. In a democratic country like America, the science of Gall and Spurzheim was too esoteric. If phrenology was to be made common coin, it must be debased; to become general knowledge it must be simplified and made practical, to appeal to the common man it must become common itself. So theory gave way to results, principles to efficiency, idealism to pragmatism. Fortified by certainty and diluted by matters of general interest, the abstruse discipline of Europe had become in America just another applied science.

Chapter 5. Controversy

The most exacting phrenologist cannot complain of any deficiency of notice of his favorite science by literati and savants, zealots and bigots, within the past year.

Eclectic Journal of Medicine, 1836

The treatment with which phrenology met, at its first announcement, both in this country and Europe, was unjust, and disgraceful to the age. It was held up to scorn and derision, and characterized by every epithet of reproach which the vocabulary of contempt could furnish. Even its amiable advocates were subjects of ridicule and persecution. . . . One might suppose that the world had learned a lesson from the opposition to Columbus and to Copernicus, and the persecutions of Galileo, and the martyrdom of Servetus.

Edward Thomson, 1856

THROUGH public lectures, the activities of the phrenological societies, and the circulation of the *American Phrenological Journal,* the new psychology achieved wide public notice in the United States. But by no means all of America was converted, nor were those not impressed disposed to regard its rise with indifference or equanimity. When confronted with its doctrines, certain types of printer's ink reached a quick boiling point, and in the newspapers, magazines, and pulpits of the Middle Period it was the subject of bitter and prolonged controversy. So strong did the division of feeling become that when Combe lectured in Hartford, although the editors of the local journals attended his course they did not report it in their columns for "fear of giving offence by either approving or disapproving." [1]

1. Combe, *Notes, 3,* 121.

Phrenological history is like military history in that it can be resolved into a series of campaigns or skirmishes against condemnation or indifference. If Spurzheim first became "news" in Great Britain by the crashing review in the *Edinburgh Review* in 1815, the same year saw the *Analectic* denounce the science for Americans. Similar disapproval was reiterated four years later by the *Portfolio,* which considered the new doctrine "specious in its appearance, and of attractive invitation, and hence has been easily listened to for a short time, by gentle and simple, by the grave and the gay; but we have not heard that it has anywhere been successful in making permanent converts. It would seem on the contrary, that the distich of the poet [applied], 'Here shallow draughts intoxicate the brain, But drinking largely sobers us again.' " [2] The *Philadelphia Medical Journal* commented on this same wave of publicity: "from the ponderous tome of the Encyclopedia down to the lighter monthly periodicals, in essay moral and literary, travels, poetry, and novels, it is made the subject of serious argumentation, or playful allusion—at times, of pointed satire or coarse invective." [3] Soon the phrenologists began to accept, and almost to enjoy, this controversial aspect, as when the Boston Phrenological Society posted a $100 prize, as noted above, for the best essay attacking it. Orson Fowler's debut in print was a challenge in the "Letters to the Editor" column of the Baltimore *Chronicle* in 1835 to debate all comers on his favorite subject, and the resulting controversy with one "Vindex" went on for forty-eight pages (still preserved in pamphlet form). Here he enunciated a stylistic credo which he was to follow for almost the next half century: "to mere literary merit, and elegance of style, the author makes no pretensions. His chief effort is to present STRONG ARGUMENTS in a PERSPICUOUS MANNER. My Pole-star is TRUTH." [4]

Interestingly enough, there was little criticism of phrenology on purely medical or scientific grounds, and slight evidence that

2. *Portfolio,* 5th ser. *8* (1819), 516.
3. *Philadelphia Medical Journal, 8* (1824), 172.
4. Orson S. Fowler, *Answer to Vindex, and Other Phrenological Matter* (Baltimore, 1835), p. 4.

such as there was accomplished very much. On the contrary, the vast majority of the indictments, and the most effective, were not rational or scientific but emotional condemnations of its philosophy and its implications. Just as the positivist today looks at religious miracles or psychic research, so did phrenology's critics dogmatically assert that not only was it untrue because it was unproven, but it couldn't be true—and it was immoral as well as foolish to assert it. If phrenology were confirmed, they said, then so were atheism, fatalism, materialism, and the denial of moral responsibility.

At the same time the phrenologists defended their doctrines not upon scientific grounds but upon irrational ones. They disregarded the original tentative and experimental nature of phrenology, did no more research, extrapolated conjecture on top of hypothesis; the fairly cautious deductions of Gall and Spurzheim were accepted as dogma and gospel, for which they became publicists and zealots. Phrenology had become not so much a science as a cult, whose advocates were "missionaries," who had received a "call," conducted "revivals," and distributed "tracts." Anyone who refused to accept conversion they characterized as either an obscurantist or an ignoramus, while they modestly compared themselves as inductive scientists to Bacon and Newton or, as martyrs, to Galileo and Bruno.

It was appropriate that the *North American Review,* in prestige at least the leading American publication, should fire the first salvo with a twenty-five page article in July, 1833. It condescended to review the subject because it had "occupied a great deal of the public attention," its adherents dividing the world into three classes: "converts, the ignorant, and persecutors." Disclaiming any prejudice, it went on to say that phrenology was anatomically unproven, involved an "ultra-Epicureanism" which proved that guilt was impersonal and crime merely a form of insanity, constituted "a quackery which succeeds by boldness," whose advocates, except for George Combe, were deficient in learning and accuracy; "since there is no evidence of the truth of phrenology, and a good deal in favor of Christianity, we incline to prefer the latter." [5] The Boston *Christian Examiner* joined the chorus with "The Pretensions of Phrenology Examined":

> The beautiful region of mental philosophy is to be converted into a barren *Golgotha,* or place of sculls. Yes! this ignoble doctrine, born of the dissecting knife and a lump of medulla, betraying at every step its mean extraction,—this carnal philosophy, with its limited conceptions, its gray truisms, its purblind theories, its withering conclusions, and its weary dogmatism is to supplant the lofty faith of antiquity, and the sublime philosophy of the Bible, and to sit in judgement on the Infinite and Eternal! . . . These powers, those thoughts, are the products of little lumps of flesh, measuring each an inch in diameter, weighing, altogether, about two pounds avoirdupois. Behold here the true nature and the full dimensions of the human soul! [6]

One clergyman thought he divined the ancestry and purpose of phrenology rather more exactly than had the *Examiner:* "Phrenology, as a science, is French materialism. All its devotees are Deists and Atheists. They can't be anything else. It reduces the mind to the mere accidental shape of the head. All the phrenologists ought to be avoided as a mortal pestilence. Their secret purpose is to subvert all religion and morals—all free agency and volition. They reduce man to a mere machine—and woman to a silly toy. . . . Avoid phrenologists as worse than the French infidels." [7]

This same religious line of attack continued in the publication of the Methodist Episcopal Church, the *Ladies' Repository,* which maintained that this doctrine would pardon impenitence with the "potent though miserable excuse" that "his *bumps* were against his being pious," and the criminal might plead the same defense; "man is to look upon himself as a mere machine, operated by forces concealed within his head . . . governed by a sort of fatality,

5. *North American Review,* 37 (1833), 80.

6. *Christian Examiner, 17* (1834), 254.

7. Quoted in *Boston Investigator,* Oct. 16, 1835, which is quoted in Albert Post, *Popular Freethought in America, 1825–1850* (New York, 1942), pp. 75–6.

over which we have no control." Since this was written in 1847, another charge could be made: once phrenology was espoused by men of science and integrity, but "in the hands of the Fowlers and many other itinerant self-seekers, it has degenerated to the reputation of a humbug. . . . Alas for phrenology, its best friends, like the murderers of Caesar, gave it the death-strokes of their own daggers." [8] Variations upon this theme of infidelity occupied a whole book when the Reverend Nathan Lewis Rice published four lengthy indictments of the science delivered in his Central Presbyterian Church of Cincinnati.[9]

Dr. David M. Reese, a choleric physician of New York, attributed charlatanry rather than infidelity to the practical phrenologist and included a chapter on this new phenomenon in his little book, *The Humbugs of New York:*

> The moral aspect of phrenological doctrines is that, however, which renders the humbug the most mischievous and deplorable. Multitudes go to the science for the purpose of easing a loaded conscience, by learning that their delinquencies and vices are constitutional, and depending wholly on organization. Such find a false peace—an imaginary comfort in the doctrine, that virtue and vice are alike the result of organs implanted by the Creator, and thus persuade themselves into the disbelief of human accountability. . . . But we must not call this materialism or fatalism, else a hue and cry of persecution is raised, as though the sympathy of heaven and earth should be moved in behalf of this humbug.[10]

Agreeing with Reese's attitude was Professor (of Mathematics) John Byrne, who published a little volume, *Anti-phrenology or, a Chapter on Humbug,* at Washington in 1843, this "to be followed" by a work on "the fallacy of restricted trade and monopoly." The

8. *Ladies' Repository,* 7 (1847), 30–1.

9. Nathan L. Rice, *Phrenology Examined, and Shown to be Inconsistent with the Principles of Physiology, Mental and Moral Science and the Doctrines of Christianity* (Cincinnati, 1849), 318 pp.

10. David M. Reese, *The Humbugs of New York* (New York, 1838), pp. 75–6.

Cazenovia *Eagle* made a similar diagnosis of the phrenologists (until Orson Fowler arrived and "converted" the village) "as members of the same fanatic fraternity with the Millerites, and Bentonian gold humbuggers." [11]

The *Princeton Review* had taken a dim view from the very first, because of Spurzheim's unorthodoxy and perhaps because he had honored Yale and Harvard with his presence but ignored the third member of the trinity. Its irritated columns libeled the phrenologists as superficial charlatans rather than conscious infidels, and their audiences for their gullible minds: "the degree of popular favour which this pseudo-science has attained in the present day, is to be attributed, in part at least, to the fact, that its darkness shelters the incapacity of its professors, which does not fail to be visible in other pursuits; and that it flatters its disciples into the belief that they possess talents and excellencies of which they have no other evidence." [12] Eleven years later it was still grumbling but now considered the doctrine "exploded and effete." [13] The *American Monthly Review* of Boston, in an otherwise favorable review of *The Constitution of Man,* admitted part of this accusation by drawing a distinction between the profundities of the science itself and the vacuity of some of its advocates:

> But if phrenology is long to survive its chiefest apostle, the excellent and lamented Spurzheim, we think it is destined to suffer more abuse and degradation from being embraced by weak minds, and preached by shallow and self-sufficient pretenders than any other system on man and mind that was ever broached. Multitudes that would never dream of embracing any system which they supposed to require profound, searching, and unwearied thought . . . will eagerly snatch at phrenology as opening a royal road, easy and short, into the very depth of metaphysics and morals . . . will believe they have nothing to do in order to be wiser than the wisest but to measure skulls and mould plaster of Paris. [14]

11. *American Phrenological Journal, 5* (1842–43), 275.
12. *Biblical Repertory and Princeton Review, 14* (1838), 320.
13. *Ibid., 21* (1849), 298.
14. *American Monthly Review, 3* (1833), 422.

One of the most striking features of the new psychology was the manner in which it was rapidly extrapolated from limited anatomical deductions into an encyclopedic system of social thought which had a recommendation (and a reform) for every facet of human life. The *North American Review* thought the keystone had nothing to do with the arch:

[Its sectaries] appear to us to have picked up by casual association with well-informed persons, a mass of odds and ends of information, which they have engrafted upon their system, without much solicitude about their exact fitness. They have been at the feast of learning and stolen the scraps.

The convenient paganism of ancient Rome, in her march towards universal dominion, took care, that the worshipper everywhere should find his own Deity among the gods of the empire. And in like manner this doctrine is ready to adopt whatever anybody happens to think wise and interesting and call it phrenology, careless so long as a multitude can be found to throw their caps in the air at the word of their leader, whether they know or believe the peculiar doctrines, whether they worship the hawk-billed divinities of Dendera, or the Jupiter of the Capitol.[15]

That brilliant scholar-statesman Caleb Cushing mined this lode, too, in disdain for reform's enthusiasms: "metaphysics are not phrenology. Ethics are not phrenology. Education, physical and mental, is not phrenology." He had read that "a celebrated professor of phrenology entertained the good people of Philadelphia with a lecture on the evils of *tight lacing*. Is that phrenology? . . . phrenology is the perversion of physiology, as alchemy is of chemistry, astrology of astronomy, and mesmerism of electromagnetism."[16] Comparable to Cushing was John Quincy Adams, another hard-headed Yankee who refused to take the new system seriously; he felt, as did Cicero about the Roman augurs, he could not see how two phrenologists could look each other in the face without bursting into laughter. Oliver Wendell Holmes, of the same breed and point of view, read a sarcastic lecture to the

15. *North American Review, 37* (1833), 83.
16. *National Magazine and Republican Review, 1* (1839), 253-4.

"boarders" at his Breakfast Table on this "pseudo-science." [17]

Each one of these attacks was duly noted, discussed, and commented on by the new sect, and if it was worthy of retort, point by point refuted. It is difficult to avoid the impression that its partisans rather expected these assaults and on the whole enjoyed the ensuing scrimmages; to quote one belligerent zealot: "The more it [phrenology] is persecuted, the brighter will it shine, and the more powerful will its effects be upon mankind. Fight on, then, ye anti-lovers of scientific truth; ye narrow-minded, sectarian worshippers; ye blind leaders of the blind. Fill your Reviews, Repositories, Journals, Advocates, Observers, and Messengers, with red-hot objection balls; fire whenever and wherever an opportunity presents itself." [18]

Just as Spurzheim had hastened to Edinburgh to confront his hostile reviewer, so the first article in the first issue of the *Annals of Phrenology* was a 102-page rebuttal of the *North American Review*. The author, as might be expected, was Charles Caldwell, whose motto was *nemo nos impune lacessit,* and his rejoinder follows the familiar Caldwell recipe of seasoning medical rhetoric with a generous amount of unbridled invective. So important was the *North American Review* regarded that even the *Phrenological Journal* of Edinburgh devoted ten pages to a detailed rejoinder. The second volume of the *Annals of Phrenology* opened with a sixty-seven-page confutation of the *Christian Examiner,* while Caldwell published separately ninety-three pages of his own animadversions on the *Christian Examiner* and its ideas. Orson Fowler, apparently on the theory that any advertising is good advertising, used to reprint verbatim attacks upon himself and his science, including paragraph by paragraph answers often longer than the original statements. When Dr. John Augustine Smith brought out his *Select Discourses against Phrenology,* the Secretary of the New York Phrenological Society, Dr. Andrew Boardman, retorted with three successive articles in the *Phrenological Journal,* which together with added illustrations later became a

17. *Writings of Oliver Wendell Holmes* (13 vols. Boston, Riverside edition, 1891), 2, 195–202.

18. Letter signed "Lover of Truth," in *American Phrenological Journal, 10* (1848), 70.

222-page book. Dr. Nathan Lewis Rice was answered promptly by one of phrenology's most notable (or notorious) controversialists, Dr. Joseph Rodes Buchanan, who presented, according to the *Cincinnati Eclectic Journal;* "our first defence"; and his address to an immense audience, in the words of the *Cincinnati Times,* "was one of the severest, most gentlemanly, and courteous specimens of 'skinning alive' that we ever witnessed." [19]

As a general rule, however, the response from the press seems to have been one of interest and sympathy, sometimes tempered with reservations. A controversial reform which was being persecuted by conservatives—that was enough for most liberal periodicals. In 1840 the *Knickerbocker* already saw forthcoming victory: "The choicest flowers of vituperation, the most subtle argument and witty sarcasm have all been unavailing. The often slain now flourishes, to all appearance, in the fulness of youthful vigour, and in the calmness of conscious strength. And why has phrenology stood thus unshaken amid the storm of opposition? Simply because it is founded on a rock—the rock of nature." [20] Timothy Flint, romantic defender of lost causes, was also cordial in his *Western Monthly Magazine:*

> There are hundreds standing ready to cry out against the advocates of the new doctrine, but the seeker after truth they dare not openly oppose. . . . It has been argued that phrenology leads to materialism, atheism, and immorality. . . . The doctrine has been called absurd, ridiculous, childish, and degrading; it has been treated in a way that casts shame upon the assailants; in short it has been attacked by argument, ridicule, and invective, notwithstanding all which, it still lives, and is still believed.[21]

The *Southern Literary Messenger* was consistently in its favor and called even such an eminent scientist as Pierre Flourens "a canting reviler of Gall," [22] while its geographical counterpart and predecessor, the *Southern Review,* had hailed it as early as 1828.

19. Quoted in *ibid.,* pp. 98–9.
20. Quoted in *ibid.,* 2 (1839–40), 480.
21. *Western Monthly Magazine, 1* (1833), 133–4.
22. *Southern Literary Messenger, 12* (1846), 272.

The *New York Mirror* reiterated its support and found that it preferred the works of the Fowlers to Gall's and Spurzheim's, since
they treated the subject "in a more useful and practical manner,"
not to mention the fact that "its arguments and principles have a
strictly moral tendency." [23] The aid and comfort of Horace Greeley's *New Yorker* and *New York Tribune* have already been mentioned. The *Ariel* of Philadelphia thought it was a discovery
worth as much as the mariner's compass or the steam engine, yet
"the universe is going to sleep over it," [24] while the *Family Magazine* did yeoman work in phrenological publicity also. Reversing
the direction of a great deal of humor which had been aimed at the
new science, *Burton's Gentleman's Magazine* went so far as to
parody the objections of Dr. David M. Reese—"the brain is really
a pudding," etc. To the *American Phrenological Review* this was
a new form of wit in a deadly serious business, so it missed the
joke completely in the inevitable retort. *Arthur's Ladies' Magazine,* a long term supporter, was complaining by 1845 that "although phrenology is now pretty generally believed, it is by no
means generally acted upon," [25] while the *Ladies' Magazine* of
Boston and the *Boston Literary Magazine* continued to recom-
mend it in their columns.

Sometimes the endorsements were not unqualified, and some
editors were perspicacious enough to analyze the all-embracing
discipline into its component parts. The *New England Magazine*
found grave objections to some of its tenets but felt it was not yet
fully developed and that there was much truth in it; as early as
1829 the *American Journal of Education* was giving a rather reserved endorsement. The Reverend Alexander Campbell, an adversary of the Reverend Nathan Lewis Rice and the founder of
the Disciples of Christ, agreed with Rice when he attacked phrenology, along with hypnotism and spirit rappings, before the
Washington Literary Society; but he said it was not phrenology
itself he was opposed to but its materialistic and infidel philosophy.
Orestes Brownson had been an auditor of both Spurzheim and

23. *New York Mirror, 14* (1837), 247.
24. *Ariel, 5* (1832), 388.
25. *Arthur's Ladies' Magazine, 4* (1845), 158.

Combe, but free soul that he was, was not so impressed by them as by his own observations. He was prepared to admit their discipline as a physical science but not a metaphysical one; its advocates should stick to their cabinets, study like physiologists, stop perambulating, and return to a sound spiritual philosophy. This reproof, that notably unhumble soul hoped, they would bear "with the meekness of philosophers." [26]

In a prescientific age the scientific journals, especially when edited by men of known integrity, had acquired extraordinary authority in reviewing new theories, and this was one of the reasons why the attack upon Spurzheim by the *Edinburgh Review* was so successful. Therefore, of all the endorsements given by men of eminence, the one most prized by the phrenologists was that of Professor Benjamin Silliman, who thought so well of his congratulatory speech after George Combe's lectures in New Haven that he published it in his *American Journal of Science* and as a pamphlet. These remarks were promptly and proudly reprinted by the *American Phrenological Journal* and the Edinburgh *Phrenological Journal*. After four different series of lectures on the subject, Silliman was convinced that "it involves no absurdity, nor any antecedent improbability. . . . is neither an unreasonable, an unphilosophical, nor an immoral or irreligious pursuit. . . . stands exactly like the other sciences of observation, upon the basis of phenomena, and their observed correspondence with a theory which is deduced from them. . . . sufficient to justify particular courses of treatment with the insane, with felons, and (with great care and prudence) even with pupils and children." [27]

This was an age of controversy and invective, and discounting most of the violent language, a general verdict would be that, all in all, the phrenological movement received "a good press." There is no evidence that this censure or ridicule hastened the new science to its early end: "any news was good news," and as long as it was in the public eye, it was growing. It was not its professed enemies but the growing eccentricities of its friends that brought it down; its failure to advance ultimately created not opposition but indifference.

26. *Boston Quarterly Review, 2* (1839), 228.
27. *American Journal of Science, 39* (1840), 87.

PART TWO. PHRENOLOGY AND AMERICAN CULTURE

Chapter 6. Phrenology and Education

No science is capable of a greater number or variety of applications than that of phrenology.

American Phrenological Journal, 1841

Either from its peculiar adaptation, or from adventitious circumstances, phrenology appears to be identified with the cause of education.

Thomas W. Olcott, 1840

ALTHOUGH phrenology was typical of the agencies which have "practically recoloured our mentality," it is hardly one of Whitehead's examples of the "quiet life of science." [1] The reason for the great popular controversy was that its protagonists had moved from its medical and scientific aspects to immediate and fundamental issues—had descended into the arena to fight mundane battles. Upon the physiological studies of Gall had been erected a mighty superstructure variously termed a social science, a universal philosophy, a guide to reform life itself; in this way the new discipline was more than just another reform, although it embraced many reforms within its compass, and its most striking feature was its optimism, its environmentalism, its hope for improvement. Its opponents, on the other hand, charged that it was of no utility, that its results were nowhere apparent; to quote the *North American Review*, "it is all promise and no performance— all action and no go." [2] This was bitterly denied by its partisans, who considered it a science of universal utility which could be applied to all phases of human affairs, one which was accomplishing

1. Alfred North Whitehead, *Science and the Modern World* (New York, 1925), p. 3.
2. *North American Review*, 37 (1833), 83.

significant reforms in American life, both through its professed
advocates and through unacknowledged borrowers.

There was no field in which the phrenologist took more interest than in education, since from his point of view an undesirable citizen was simply one whose mental organs had not developed properly; a vice was nothing more than a faculty which was
overdeveloped or underdeveloped.[3] This could be corrected and
a proper phrenological organization attained by the proper
therapy, i.e. by the doctrine of the growth of the faculties by
exercise (or diminution by disuse). As one speaker put it, to the
despondent the voice of psychology whispers, "Your *organism*
and *not* your *fate,* is at fault." [4] But prevention is better than
cure; more logical, as well as easier, would be a proper course
of education from the cradle up. As Dr. William Elder, Philadelphia's noted physician and economist, wrote for the *American
Phrenological Journal,* the moral and social evils existing in
society were dependent upon a wrong system of education,
wrong because it was not in harmony with nature and did not
develop the physical, intellectual, and moral nature of man; a
correct system of education would do this and consequently reform and renovate the world.[5]

Thus it was that all the famous proponents of the new psy-
chology, always with the exception of the scientist Gall, took
deep interest in, gave detailed lectures, and wrote books on the
aims and techniques of education. Spurzheim's *Education, Its
Elementary Principles Founded on the Nature of Man,* George
Combe's *Lectures on Popular Education,* Orson Fowler's *Education and Self-improvement* and *The Perfection of Character,
Including the Management of Youth,* and Charles Caldwell's
*Thoughts on the True Mode of Improving the Condition of
Man* are only a few of the works which appeared in American
editions on the subject.

The theses of these various books are remarkably consistent

3. The faculty of Combativeness, for example, if underdeveloped would
result in timidity; if overdeveloped, belligerence.
4. Sizer, *Forty Years in Phrenology,* p. 246.
5. *American Phrenological Journal, 13* (1850), 15.

and run something like this: the mind cannot function without the brain, and the brain is intimately connected with the body; therefore a healthy body is a necessity and is to be obtained by following the laws of physiology and health. Constant mental exercise at an early age can only succeed in weakening the brain permanently; so children should not be encouraged to be mental prodigies but should have plenty of physical training. They must have a short school day rather than a long one, with a great deal of play and fresh air. Instead of forcing and drilling the child, the teacher with a knowledge of phrenology should attempt to understand the individual pupil and to encourage right actions by rewards instead of wrong ones by punishments, all the while varying and alternating subjects to prevent boredom. Students should be allowed "all the liberty in their training that they can take without abusing it. . . . It begets in them the spirit of independence and self-reliance and self-government . . . induces them to think on their own responsibility, and to feel that they are accountable for their conduct." [6] Pupils should be taught objects rather than words and learn words as a whole rather than by individual letters; they should learn by doing instead of by remembering, by concrete illustration rather than abstract reasoning. Questions should be encouraged and answered. Studies should be practical and concrete in place of such abstract and useless subjects as Greek and Latin. If the brain were a single mental organ, then exercise of any sort would be beneficial to the whole, and therefore concentration upon the classics would actually train the whole mind, as it claimed to. But in actuality the mind was a congeries of organs—a piano, not a trumpet—and thus these differing aptitudes should be exercised individually. Study of the classics, then, trains the faculty of language but no more. The aims and techniques of phrenology applied to education, taken as a whole, sound today remarkably like those of twentieth-century "progressive education"—and in an age of the three *R's* and the hickory stick they sounded radical indeed.[7]

6. *Ibid.*, 25 (1857), 87.

7. The parallelism between certain phrenological educational theories— the education of the child through his own voluntary activity, the develop-

The administration of such a curriculum, of course, was dependent on the professional teachers, but according to this new doctrine, of equal importance was the role of the mother; like Freudianism, it maintained that the crucial years were those of infancy. Orson Fowler went so far as to say: "Reason without fact can teach very little. . . . By a law of mind, observation must PRECEDE reasoning. . . . This inductive method of gaining knowledge appertains to the juvenile even more than to the adult. . . . Even before children are three months old, crowd OBJECTS upon their notice. . . . instead of chiding them, take special pains to explain all, and even to excite curiosity to know still more." [8] And that is the reason Mrs. Sarah J. Hale, the editor of Boston's *Ladies' Magazine,* had urged attendance at Spurzheim's lectures—the "necessity of female participation in the science." [9] After his death she ran his eulogy in black borders and maintained that "excepting Christianity, phrenology will do more to elevate woman than any other system has ever done. It gives her a participation in the labors of mind. She must understand its principles and practice them in the nursery. And her influence it is which must mould the minds of her children and improve the world." [10] It was on this ground that a considerable number of phrenological works on the raising of children was absorbed by the American public and quoted by other writers on child education, particularly Samuel Goodrich and Homan Humphrey.

In magazines devoted to a more professional audience the same educational doctrines were publicized and enthusiastically seconded. The *American Annals of Education* was cordial to Spurzheim's *Principles of Education,* if somewhat critical of his

---

ment of inborn faculties by arousing interest and exercise—and the theories of Pestalozzi and Froebel is evident. Since the phrenologists never cited these great Europeans, obviously the assimilation was indirect, unconscious, and a result of "the spirit of the times."

8. Orson S. Fowler, *Memory and Intellectual Improvement Applied to Self-education and Juvenile Instruction* (New York, 1883), pp. 44–5.

9. *Ladies' Magazine,* 5 (1832), 474.

10. *Ibid.,* 6 (1833), 572.

casual religion; it quoted Andrew Combe at length and noted in vague irritation "it is not the phrenologist alone, who talks of the evils of our hot bed systems." [11] The very word phrenology, on the other hand, is totally obliterated from the pages of the *American Journal of Education;* Henry Barnard, although a friend of George Combe and a sponsor of his lectures, wished to avoid controversy and censored the subject, and remarks for or against, out of the magazine he started in 1855. The columns of the *American Phrenological Journal* were filled with letters from enthusiastic school teachers: *"no rod or rule—*those relics of atrocious barbarity—are admitted in the government and discipline; nothing but the purest quintessence of phrenology, guides me." [12] Or this pedagogue, recently arrived in Muscatine, Iowa: "I have not had an occasion to resort to corporeal punishment. . . . In fact, I have not 'whipped a scholar,' in near eighteen months, since I attended your course of lectures in Syracuse, New York. I owe my success mainly to the little knowledge I have of phrenology." [13] "A noted agent for improving the common schools in Pennsylvania" derived his ideas and his fame from Spurzheim's works. Timothy Flint's essays on education came from the same source.[14]

Not only did the question arise, should teaching be conducted according to phrenological principles, but also should phrenology itself be taught in the schools as a regular subject? This need was foreseen by Mrs. Lorenzo Fowler, who wrote a series of simple question-answer type books—*Familiar Lessons Designed for the Use of Children and Youth in Schools and Families*—on phrenology, hygiene, and astronomy, an effort highly commended by the *American Journal of Insanity;* [15] the Albany Phrenological Society had already arranged for an edition of *The Constitution of Man* in a similar format for the same purpose. William L. Crandal in his *Three Hours School a Day: a Talk with Parents* ad-

11. *American Annals of Education,* 7 (1837), 171.
12. *American Phrenological Journal,* 4 (1842), 140.
13. *Ibid., 14* (1851), 66.
14. *Ibid., 6* (1844), 41–2; *Western Monthly Review, 3* (1830), 393–402.
15. *American Journal of Insanity, 5* (1848–49), 280–1.

vised the purchase of Combe's *The Constitution of Man* and a
copy of his *Phrenology,* to "learn there the foundation of the
Science of Education"; [16] Crandal's book, being written under
the right star, was hailed by the *American Phrenological Journal*
as "the most remarkable work published since *The Constitution
of Man.*" [17]

In a fine flush of enthusiasm one of the assistant editors of the
American Phrenological Journal, B. J. Gray, purchased a set of
buildings at Eatontown, New Jersey, for a school in which phrenology would not merely be offered as a single subject—as it was
in the Cincinnati high schools or the Boston School for Moral
Discipline—but rather the whole establishment would be run on
strictly phrenological principles, with shower baths, gymnasium,
lectures on physiology "illustrated with the Manikin," excursions
to the beach, and appeals to the higher faculties. But two years
later, in 1848, Mr. Gray made the laconic announcement that he
was returning to the lecturing field; apparently the Eatontown
Institute was not sustained.

George Combe, in addition to devoting two lectures of his regular course to education, used to give a short series in places where
he had neither the time nor guarantee for the full sixteen lectures,
and in this abbreviated course three were on the application of his
science to education. So much interest was awakened by these that
he gave them again and again, until "I received more invitations
to repeat these lectures than it was possible for me to comply
with." [18] The whole month of December, 1839, was devoted to this
set, delivered to the teachers of Boston in the Odeon, again to
the subscribers in the Lyceum with 1500 in attendance, and then
in Salem, Lowell, Worcester, and Springfield. Henry Barnard, who
"entertains enlightened views on the subject of education," [19] was
anxious to have him deliver his addresses on the philosophy of
phrenology and its application to education for his Hartford Young
Men's Institute, and paid part of his fee from the lecture fund of

16. (Albany, 1854), p. 87.
17. *American Phrenological Journal,* 21 (1855), 141.
18. Combe, *Notes, 3,* 213.
19. *Ibid.,* p. 85.

the Institute. Combe always made a particular attempt to speak to teachers and insisted that the assistant teachers of the common schools be admitted free. The reason for this, he said, was that the United States was the nation above all which required the finest educational system; "knowledge and virtue are most needed" in a democratic social structure.

As a result of his strenuous efforts on behalf of education, Combe thought much was accomplished. On his second visit to Boston he was gratified to discover "decided proofs of the effect of his lectures delivered in the previous year": [20] there was increased interest in subjects and methods of teaching, members of the Board of Education displayed enhanced zeal in the cause, and improved schools had been built with particular provision for ventilation (his American audiences, unaccustomed to "night air," were invariably horrified when he dramatized his principles by throwing wide the windows at the intermissions of his two-hour lectures).

He also became the friend of many prominent intellectuals and educators who were interested in phrenology, such as Cyrus Peirce and George B. Emerson. But the greatest of these was Horace Mann. Combe wrote home: "Mr. Mann assures me that I am aiding him effectually, and am advancing his labours by years," [21] and it was at Mann's earnest solicitation that Combe was induced to do all the lectures on pedagogy. Just before becoming Secretary of the School Board of Massachusetts and starting upon his famous career, Mann had read *The Constitution of Man* and had become a total convert. He regarded phrenology as the greatest discovery of the ages and built all his theories of mental and moral improvement upon the ideas which it had furnished him. He lectured upon it, wrote letters in its peculiar terminology, recommended its study to young men and teachers, and referred to it in his official reports. The much criticized Sixth Report reads like a vast gloss on *The Constitution of Man* and quotes Andrew Combe four times. Consequently, when Combe first arrived at Boston in 1838, Mann became his devoted follower and warm friend. That summer he

20. Gibbon, *Combe*, 2, 75.
21. *Ibid.*

visited Combe at Cape Cod, and in the spring of 1840 they toured
the West through Ohio and Kentucky together; after Combe's
return to England a correspondence ensued that lasted all their
lives, in which Mann wrote "there is no man who has done me so
much good as you have. I see many of the most valuable truths
as I never should have seen them but for you, and all truths better
than I should otherwise have done," [22] and added the ultimate compliment, that he was naming a son after him. Combe replied from
Edinburgh, "I shall rejoice to sow seeds which Mr. Mann may
ripen into a lovely and abundant harvest of morality and intelligence." [23]

The educational principles applicable to the training of normal children could also be applied to all varieties of defectives.
Dr. Samuel Gridley Howe, an old crusader for lost causes at home
as well as in Greece, had been a confidant of Spurzheim and Corresponding Secretary, President, and frequent speaker at the Boston
Phrenological Society. He, too, became a close and lifelong friend,
and Julia Ward Howe has left an unforgettable description of
the two of them strolling through the Vatican galleries looking
at Greek sculpture heads for confirmation of their favorite science.
At the time Howe first became acquainted with the new psychology
he volunteered for the position of first superintendent of the new
Boston School for the Blind and began the career for which he
is remembered in history; against great obstacles of ignorance and
pessimism he demonstrated to the world that these unfortunates
could and should be educated to be socially and economically competent, largely through methods of his own devising. As Combe
wrote, "Dr. Howe has a bold, active, enterprising mind, and to a
certain extent he impresses his own character on the minds of his
pupils. He enlarges the practical boundaries of their capacities by
encouraging them to believe in the greatness of their natural extent." [24] Howe had an outline of phrenology and *The Constitution
of Man* printed in raised type, in his opinion "the most valuable

22. B. A. Hinsdale, *Horace Mann and the Common School Revival in
the United States* (New York, 1898, reprinted 1937), p. 95.
23. Gibbon, *Combe*, 2, 44.
24. Combe, *Notes*, 3, 23.

addition ever yet made to the library for the blind in any language." When Combe lectured in Boston, at Howe's request the blind pupils from his institute were admitted without charge. All his success Howe attributed to his study of phrenology:

> Before I knew phrenology, I was groping my way in the dark as blind as my pupils; I derived very little satisfaction from labours, and fear I gave but little to others. . . . Some of our teachers are persons of considerable intellectual attainments, and all of them adopted the new philosophy since they joined the institution . . . because their duties led them to examine all the theories of mental philosophy, and the new system recommended itself most forcibly to their understanding, and appeared more susceptible of practical application.[25]

George Combe used to tell in his lectures on education an anecdote about the more mundane uses to which the science might be put: Howe perceived that the fault with an ungovernable blind pupil was that the boy had large "Destructiveness," so put him to sawing wood and working out in the gymnasium before school hours, and there were no difficulties, disciplinary or otherwise, thereafter. In "the sentimental years" modesty was a cardinal virtue, and Howe used to train his students' organ of propriety by never allowing them to appear undressed within each other's "vision."

Charles Sumner had introduced Howe to the New York heiress, Julia Ward, and after their marriage she assisted in his work and recorded that phrenology was of great assistance in teaching the famous Laura Bridgman to communicate with others. This was a revolution in psychological circles, since the blind deaf-mute was previously thought to be hopeless, but the new science was an optimistic one, for it "leads us to understand that in this child Laura Bridgman the moral and intellectual powers exist in great vigour and activity, and all that is wanting to her successful education is the means of conveying knowledge to them." [26] George Combe was so interested in this vindication of his teachings that he carried on a transatlantic correspondence over her case with

25. *Ibid.,* p. 86.
26. *Ibid.,* p. 187.

her mentor, subscribed to the fund for her training, and included a special appendix on her in his *Notes on the United States*.

Phrenology had made Howe such an optimist that he once declared in an official report that even oysters were capable of improvement. When he read that James Simpson, an Edinburgh phrenologist, had succeeded in educating an idiot boy, he investigated that subject and established at Boston in 1848 the first school in the world for those unfortunates. But he was by no means the only member of his psychological fraternity who was active in reclaiming the handicapped. Thomas Hopkins Gallaudet, the Connecticut pioneer and first principal of the Hartford School for the Deaf and Dumb, was a believer in phrenology and a friend and cicerone to George Combe. Silas Jones had been a writer on phrenology and a traveling lecturer prior to his appointment as head of the New York Asylum for the Blind in 1838. Adept these leaders were in devising new techniques for teaching the unfortunate, and always they were certain that it *could* be done: "a knowledge of physiology, of human and comparative anatomy, and of *educability* in its widest sense, are requisite to form a phrenologist." [27]

27. Howe, *Address*, p. 17.

Chapter 7. Phrenology and Insanity

It is indeed, too true, that the ignorance of the philosophy of the human mind, and of its relations to the brain as its material organ, is one of the greatest obstacles, not only to the present cure of the insane, but to the farther advancement of our medical knowledge of insanity; and till this truth shall be recognized in its fullest force, and the principles of phrenology be adopted as the physiological . . . basis of a mental philosophy, we shall look in vain for those ameliorations in the management of the insane which are so imperatively required.

Andrew Combe, 1834

THE PHRENOLOGISTS took a particular interest in insanity, which they regarded as their own province of psychiatry, and it was a standard avocation of the phrenological societies to tour insane asylums and comment learnedly on the unusual specimens therein. For them the insane represented the pathological exaggeration of normal traits which could thereby be studied more easily; to understand the normal we must explore the abnormal. According to the humanitarian and optimistic tenets of this humane science, the insane were unfortunates who should be helped and reformed; and by following the same phrenological theories of brain structure, education, and therapy, this type of defective could be educated and mental disease cured.

Until the beginning of the 19th century there had been almost no advance in either the theory or treatment of insanity. Under the then prevalent theories of metaphysical psychology the mind had been regarded as a single unit and as ethereal in essence, a sort of immaterial emanation from the Creator. When a person lost his sanity, he was considered by the religiously minded as literally possessed by evil spirits, and by all he was thought to have retrogressed to the animal level, insensitive to human stimuli and undeserving of humane treatment, which explains the abysmal cruelty of 18th-century bedlams as well as the brutal treatment meted out even to George III in his frequent seizures. Insanity was regarded as a sort of dread visitation, to be concealed as a source of shame to the family; the medical profession considered it a waste of time to minister to it, since the only obvious therapy was to try literally to frighten the patient into lucidity or at least submission by ice baths or "snake pits." While the Europeans Tuke and Pinel and the American Dorothea Dix proposed to mitigate this barbarous regimen, they did so on purely humanitarian and empirical grounds.

Phrenology, on the other hand, proposed in place of this vacuous superstition a completely rationalistic, plausible, consistent explanation, which left no questions unanswered. The new psychology's basic assumptions, which seemed relatively novel at the time, was that the brain was the organ of mind, and following the analogy of nature, therefore a diseased condition of the mind, i.e. insanity, indicated a diseased brain. Insanity was a symptom of a corporeal disease, not a visitation from the Lord—it was as delirium to a fever, or fever to a disease, or red spots to the measles. It was the disease and not the symptom which should be treated, and the instrument was phrenology, which in the words of the *American Journal of Insanity*, "bears the same relation to insanity that physiology does to pathology." [1] In other words, instead of the prevalent psychic theory and empirical treatment, here was a completely physical theory which held that insanity could be treated as a rational branch of medicine and according to the same principles as, for example, a disease of the liver or lungs; in fact, it was now termed "cerebral medicine" or "cerebral pathology." [2]

1. *American Journal of Insanity, 6* (1849), 128.

2. In all justice to the phrenologists it should be pointed out that while no one treats insanity today according to the theories of phrenology (although its practices, empirically, *were* generally sound), the question of the origin and nature of insanity remains unsettled, and it would be a foolhardy historian who ventured into that torn battleground between the psychoanalysts and the advocates of shock treatment.

To say that insanity was a disease of the brain did not mean, of course, that the whole brain was diseased, since according to the same doctrine, the brain was a congeries of organs. Usually just one or more faculties were morbid; but always, Spurzheim maintained, autopsies of the insane show evidences of disease. Again the rationale behind this hypothesis was entirely plausible; the theorists could quote the familiar phenomena of the insane—monomania, *idée fixe*, hallucinations, split personality, dreams—to suggest that not the whole mind was unsound but only certain parts of it, that the alternation between mania and lucid intervals in a madman was simply the intermittent action of diseased and healthy hemisphere or organs, that such a misfortune as nymphomania was no more than a diseased cerebellum.[3]

The causation of such affliction followed logically from the general theories. There were, of course, cases of injuries to the brain by concussions and fractures, as well as paresis (although it was not diagnosed as such until many years later). But usually insanity arose, they said, from origins which involved the basic premise that the mind is intimately connected with the body. Spurzheim divided the sources into two classifications: "sympathic," i.e. disease residing in other parts and influencing the brain—such as rheumatism, scarlet fever, diseased liver—and more frequently "idiopathic," disease in the brain itself and usually due to violation of the "natural laws of man" which phrenology stressed so heavily, like too much study in childhood, not enough fresh air or exercise, masturbation, liquor, tobacco, or too heavy concentration on religion.

The treatment of the disease varied with the individual case. The behavior of the patient and the shape of the skull, if it was unusual, were carefully observed, and it was decided what organs were at fault. Sometimes to reduce the flow of blood to that organ, "depletion" (the application of leeches) was practiced, along with hot packs, mustard plasters, or even trepanning, plus drugs and laxatives. But the best therapy was simply a course of following "the natural laws," the neglect of which had brought on the dis-

3. Technically the organ of Amativeness, located at the base of the neck.

ease: a regimen of fresh air, physical exercise, bland diet with no liquor or tobacco, plenty of rest and sleep and moral uplift, warmth, placidity, and little intellectual effort.

This new mode of treatment was to differ from its inhumane predecessor especially in its atmosphere. Spurzheim insisted upon an elaborate set of buildings and a "cottage" plan with the cases segregated according to their own alienation; the patients would be transported from their old environment with its exciting causes to a quiet, secluded, kindly one, with no chains, strait jackets, restraints, or punishments—according to phrenological doctrine, these only increased the desire to exercise the undesirable propensities and to whip such a case would make as much sense as flogging a person with indigestion. The intention was to develop the moral faculties by exercise and carefully avoid anything to stimulate the overdeveloped violent faculties, which if allowed to lie dormant would gradually return to manageable proportions.

The impact of these theories of diagnosis and treatment was both extensive and intensive upon the doctors and administrators of what passed for lunatic asylums in the America of the 1830's and 1840's. One of the most prominent was Dr. Amariah Brigham, who accompanied Spurzheim on his memorable visits to the Hartford Asylum for the Deaf and Dumb and to the State Prison at Weathersfield on his way to Boston in 1832. The next year he wrote an appendix for the American edition of Spurzheim's work on insanity, following this with three books on the relation between mental health and social activity, all in accordance with the theories of the new science. All Brigham's writing was done with wit and style, designed to appeal to the general reader, if not to Dr. David M. Reese, who was provoked to splenetic retort. Brigham took an early interest in the problem of mental derangement, which he found "very difficult to explain, except on the ground adopted by Gall and Spurzheim, and eloquently developed and illustrated by the Messrs. Combe." [4] After serving as professor of anatomy and surgery in the College of Physicians and Surgeons in New York City, he became in 1840 physician and superintend-

4. *The Influence of Mental Derangement upon Health* (Boston, 1833), pp. 27–8.

ent of the Retreat for the Insane in Hartford, where he acted as cicerone for George Combe and "pointed out a case of mania proceeding from disease of the cerebellum, which he had successfully treated by local depletion in that region." [5] In 1842 he was called to be the first superintendent of the New York State Lunatic Asylum at Utica, which he staffed with what the *American Phrenological Journal* hailed as "a phrenological regency." He used to send the Fowlers copies of his annual reports, had Lorenzo Fowler give a lecture to his several hundred charges ("they appeared highly pleased, and were very attentive auditors" [6]) and when Brigham died, the *Journal* mourned that "A GREAT AND GOOD MAN HAS FALLEN!" [7]

In 1844 Brigham and his staff founded the *American Journal of Insanity*, the first periodical in English devoted to psychiatric problems, designed for the general public as well as the specialist. This first flower of missionary zeal was eventually taken over by the American Psychiatric Association. In its second number it ran a sort of manifesto, of which this paragraph is relevant:

> we infer that the brain is not a single organ, but a congeries of organs, as maintained by the illustrious Gall and his celebrated successors Spurzheim and Combe. Thus each mental faculty has a special organ, and therefore certain faculties may be disordered by disease of the brain, while others are not affected; a fact every day observed in Lunatic Asylums, but which we know not how to explain if we believe the brain to be a single organ.[8]

The *American Journal of Insanity* thereafter had many articles on phrenology and its application to "cerebral pathology." For example, Amos Dean, Albany's famous lawyer and educator, contributed an analysis of a particular case within his observation; Dr. C. B. Coventry, Professor of Midwifery and Medical Jurisprudence at Geneva College and a member of Brigham's staff at

5. Combe, *Notes, 3*, 120.
6. *American Phrenological Journal, 10* (1848), 374.
7. *Ibid., 11* (1849), 320.
8. *American Journal of Insanity, 1* (1844–45), 105.

Utica, wrote a long article, "The Physiology of the Brain," maintaining a purely phrenological position, interestingly enough, without mentioning the word. Dr. H. A. Buttolph read a paper entitled "The Relation of Phrenology to Insanity" before the Association of Medical Superintendents of American Institutions for the Insane in May, 1851, and this was reprinted in the *American Journal of Insanity* as well as the *American Phrenological Journal*. Like Brigham, Buttolph was on cordial terms with the Fowlers, used to send them his annual reports, each year address their classes, and reported interesting cases of phrenological derangement to their *Journal*.

Taking precedence over Brigham in point of time and prestige was Dr. Samuel B. Woodward, the first head of the Massachusetts State Lunatic Asylum at Worcester, which began the movement toward state asylum building. His success in meeting the problems of custodial and remedial care of the insane occasioned nationwide comment, and his reports, circulating in editions as large as 3,000, were the most widely read and quoted in America. In 1844 he became the founder and first president of the Association of Medical Superintendents of American Institutions for the Insane (now shortened to the American Psychiatric Association), and until his retirement he "was generally regarded, both at home and abroad, as the leading American authority on mental diseases." [9] George Combe visited his sanitarium twice and found him "an enlightened phrenologist" who "expressed his surprise how any man, living in charge of a hospital for the insane, and capable of mental analysis and physical observation, reasonably acquainted with phrenology, could avoid conviction of its truth," while his sanitarium was "a noble monument of enlightened philanthropy and of excellent administration." [10] Woodward told Nahum Capen of the Boston Phrenological Society that while he resorted to "local applications" only occasionally, "it was impossible successfully to treat the insane without the aid of phrenology." [11] "His application of the new science was uniform and avowed, and the results attained by him

9. Albert Deutsch, *The Mentally Ill in America* (New York, 1937), p. 149.
10. Combe, *Notes, 1,* 57.
11. Capen, *Reminiscences,* p. 168.

have tended to promote a general and practical recognition of its principles in similar institutions throughout the United States." [12]

Another famous American alienist profoundly influenced by phrenology was Dr. Isaac Ray, one of the pioneers in this little explored field. In 1841 he was appointed medical superintendent of the State Hospital for the Insane at Augusta, Maine, and after making a two-year survey of European institutions, he designed the Butler Asylum at Providence, of which he was the head for the next twenty years. Like Drs. Brigham and Woodward, he was one of "the original thirteen" founders of the Association of the Medical Superintendents, as well as, later, its president. Not only an eminent authority in the profession, he was also probably the most intelligent and sophisticated writer on the subject of psychiatry in this country, with a biting literary skill and a mind abreast of developments in the social sciences outside his own field. In 1832 he had reviewed *The Constitution of Man* so enthusiastically for the Boston *Christian Examiner* that the editor had to insert a footnote disclaiming any endorsement.[13] His attention in 1837 was directed to the legal aspects of insanity, a juridical area almost totally ignored, and the result was a 650-page treatise entitled *The Medical Jurisprudence of Insanity*, which received wide attention and is still useful. In this he frequently quoted Gall, Spurzheim, and the two Combes. He maintained the basic phrenological position that insanity was a physical disease and always involves physical derangement of brain structures; that it should be treated as a disease and not the moral blight for which laymen in general, and judges and juries in particular, tended to punish its unfortunate victims. George Combe repaid the compliment in his *Notes on the United States* and commended the work for treating the subject on phrenological principles and for containing "much excellent matter." [14] "A giant among men of his speciality," [15] in

12. *Phrenological Journal*, *19* (1846), 386, quoting the *Popular Record of Modern Science*, August 8, 1846.

13. Perry Miller has engagingly recounted this incident in his *The Transcendentalists: an Anthology* (Cambridge, 1950), pp. 75–6.

14. Combe, *Notes*, *1*, 104.

15. G. Alden Blumer, "Isaac Ray," in *DAB*.

1863 Ray completed *Mental Hygiene,* an exposition of the origins and nature of insanity and a program for its prevention. By this time, as we shall see, the first flush of enthusiasm for phrenology had passed away, and medical men were inclined to take a close hard look at what had seemed so plain three decades before. Now the author admitted that with the exception of a few organs, the evidence for anatomical localization of the faculties of the brain "has not satisfied the deliberate and unbiased judgement of scientific men," but he still maintained that the phrenological "analysis of the mental phenomena is clear and precise, indicating—what metaphysical inquiries seldom have—a shrewd observation of the springs of action, and a profound insight of the relations of man to the sphere in which he moves"; its value lies in "having indicated the true mode of investigation, and especially for the light it throws on the whole process of education and development." [16]

Enough has been said to demonstrate that phrenology as psychiatric theory had a profound influence on the conduct of American insane asylums and that it was familiar and suggestive to workers in a field almost devoid of a theory of mind to explain what they were trying to do. The best known figure in the movement, Dorothea Dix, had no connection with phrenology. Her interest was not clinical and her motives, as has been said, were purely humanitarian; but at least she recognized George Combe's prominence in the crusade and called upon him, on her trip to Scotland, as a fellow-spirit and colleague. Other humanitarian reformers were enlisted in the crusade. Dr. Samuel Gridley Howe was an influential supporter of Dr. Woodward's institution, as well as the beneficiary of Woodward's assistance; he was tilling a corner of the same field with his Massachusetts School for Idiotic and Feeble-minded Youth. No philanthropic movement would have been complete without the support of Horace Mann, and Isaac Ray's *The Medical Jurisprudence of Insanity* was dedicated to him, "to whose persevering exertions our country is mainly indebted for one of its noblest institutions for ameliorating the condition of the insane." This last refers to Mann's valiant fight in the Massachusetts House of Representatives in 1829 and 1830 for

16. Isaac Ray, *Mental Hygiene* (Boston, 1863), p. 91.

the establishment of the Worcester Asylum, which was later called (by Howe) "Horace Mann's monument," and of which he was chairman of the board of trustees. He composed the *Sixth Annual Report* of that institution, which provides the best succinct statement of the objectives and accomplishments of the phrenological theory of insanity:

> The efforts of Dr. Woodward have effected a deep change in public opinion. They have demonstrated that insanity is a physical disease; that it has its origin in certain natural causes, being induced by a violation of some of the organic laws, upon which mental functions depend; that these causes are not mysterious and inscrutable in any peculiar sense; that they are capable of being recognized and understood, like the causes that bring on consumption or the gout; that insanity is a curable disease; that it is a disease far less dangerous to life than fevers usually are; and finally, that not only the means of cure, but the ways of prevention, in ordinary cases, have been entrusted to us, accompanied by the responsibility of rightly using them.[17]

What the alienists of the 1830's and 1840's saw in phrenology was a body of experimental knowledge and a new approach to the problem of mental disease. In later years Isaac Ray, even though he never reached much belief in cranioscopy, remembered devouring Gall's work like a "story-book"[18] because it cast a whole new light on mental science. In the decades to come these psychiatrists were to see that their brave optimism and phenomenal records of "cures" were based on inadequate diagnoses and specious statistics, and that insanity was a much more inscrutable affair than the enthusiasm of the Combes made out. Yet the rational approach and the physical regimen they prescribed remain valid today.

17. Quoted in *Christian Examiner*, 26 (1839), 248.
18. Capen, *Reminiscences*, p. 139.

Chapter 8. Phrenology and Penology

We rejoice at the establishment of the Prison Discipline Journal, and hope it will avail itself of that flood of light . . . that has been thrown upon the whole subject of crime and prison discipline by physiology and phrenology, sciences that have shown the relation between the physical constitution and the mental and moral faculties. In our opinion, the principles advanced in the works of Gall, Spurzheim, Combe, Simpson, Sampson, and others of that class, and the practical excellences of those principles, as exhibited in several Prisons in other countries, ought not to be overlooked by a Journal devoted to the improvement of Prison Discipline.

American Journal of Insanity, 1845

Policeman nothing said
   (though he had much to say on it),
But from the bad man's head
   He took the cap that lay on it.

"Observe his various bumps,
   His head as I uncover it;
His morals lie in lumps
   All round about and over it.

"For Burglars, Thieves, and Co.,
   Indeed I'm no apologist;
But I, some years ago,
   Assisted a Phrenologist."

W. S. Gilbert

FROM the care of the insane to the treatment of the criminal was a logical extension of phrenological theory. After all, according to the new doctrine, an undesirable citizen was one with an unfortunate organization of the brain, which could be corrected or at least improved by the proper application of this universal science.

The conventional theory of penology during the 18th century (has it ever changed?) was to apply such severe penalties to crime that these not only would serve as an example to potential wrong-doers but would prevent felons from repeating their misdeeds for fear of repeating their punishments; the assumption, of course, was that the mind of the criminal was constituted precisely like that of the virtuous citizen. But the phrenologists came to the eminently reasonable if unconventional conclusion that the vast majority of criminals are swayed by impulse and do not have sufficient moral sense to be inhibited by possible retribution. So society's retribution upon the criminal as an example to potential imitators serves only to make a hardened criminal of him; "culprits are but perverse and wicked children," [1] and the more they are compelled and coerced, the worse they become. The phrenologists maintained that since man's instincts are naturally good, antisocial actions are a form of insanity and should be treated in somewhat the same fashion—as a moral problem in a sort of "moral hospital." There the convict would be considered a "patient" and after a course of development of the moral faculties and avoidance of unhealthy influences could finally be discharged, not because he had paid his debt to society but because he was cured. Punishment in itself, they contended, meant little, since the prisoner was in no way a better man when he was released. Prisons should rather be rehabilitation centers—to give the criminal good treatment, a proper education, and new incentives. The basic principles would be those of humane consideration and a pity for moral ignorance and infirmity, the remedy that of giving the "patient" healthy surroundings, making him feel that his own comfort could be attained only by honest conduct, and presenting him the prospect of an honorable future. Vindictive punishment not only is unworthy of the humanitarianism of an enlightened age but is useless. A crime can only mean a disordered organization of the brain, since the instincts of a healthy brain can only be good. Society is inconsistent in treating this disorder in a different manner from any other disease, i.e. by restraint, seclusion, care, and if

1. *Phrenological Journal,* 7 (1831–32), 501.

possible, cure, but it is the decision of society whether this therapy shall be in a mental hospital or a penitentiary.[2]

About the practical measures necessary to implement this theoretical framework the phrenologists occasionally differed slightly among themselves, but George Combe's program was the best known. He found the two much-discussed innovations of America—the so-called "congregate" system practiced at New York's Auburn Prison and Pennsylvania's "solitary" system—steps in the right direction but lacking "sufficient means for strengthening the moral and intellectual faculties of the prisoners," [3] even though he incorporated the basic features of both in his regimen. The ordinary criminal should be classified phrenologically and given an indeterminate sentence; he would begin by solitary confinement and gradually be permitted labor and an intensive course in moral, intellectual, and religious instruction. As repentance and the desire for reformation became manifest, the seclusion and severe discipline could be relaxed. Then his moral faculties could be exercised by permitting association with convicts of his same classification and stage of regeneration, and the more powers of virtuous conduct he displayed, the more liberty he should be awarded, eventually being allowed occasional trips away from the prison on parole. Finally, he could be released.

Combe saw another virtue in his plan, that those unfit for return to society would never make the grade. He thought his investigations revealed another class of criminal, in whom the intellect and moral sentiments were so small and the propensities so large that their tendency was almost irresistibly toward evil, and these he defined as "morally insane" or what we would call today incorrigibles. But this was distinctly against the reform cur-

2. "From disturbance of the harmonious action of the different organs and functions of the brain, there results that which physicians name mental disease, theologians sin, and lawyers crime. Every crime arises from the abnormal action of one or more cerebral organs. Every crime, therefore, is an act of insanity as well as a sin. The discordant action of the mental functions may be treated by three different means—punishment, penance, and medicine. . . . Crime is disease, but disease is not crime." Dr. Attomyr, *Theory of Crimes, based on the Principles of Phrenology* (Leipzig, 1842), quoted in Edinburgh *Phrenological Journal, 16* (1843), 259.

3. *Phrenological Journal, 16* (1843), 15.

rent of the time, the belief that all men were equal and the religious conviction of salvation for all; Dorothea Dix's proposals met legislative approval because these asylums proposed (and provided statistical "proof" of ability) to *cure* the insane. "If his [Combe's] lectures had stimulated scientific research rather than righteous indignation, he might have antedated the Italian Lombroso as the founder of modern penology." [4]

While the accomplishments in prison reforms, of course, were not so striking as those in education and the care of the insane, the application of phrenology to penology was extensively discussed in America, and in some cases acted upon. Charles Caldwell, as usual, was first in the New World to project the guide lines marked out by Gall and Spurzheim, in his *New Views of Penitentiary Discipline* (Lexington, 1827). Like Spurzheim, George Combe was an indefatigable explorer of American jails, which he visited in company with public officials and the officers of the various phrenological societies along his route. He made an intensive study of them, concentrating on Sing Sing, exhibited by Governor William H. Seward, and the Pennsylvania State Prison, since these were the laboratories of the new theories which were agitating the penologists' world. His observations and criticisms of the reformatories fill a large portion of his *Notes on the United States,* and his own views on the subject were summarized in one of the lectures in his oft-repeated course. The repercussions of these lectures and writings, and of the agitation of the phrenological societies, are indicated by letters to Combe from American friends: "the officers of the prisons in this State [N.Y.] are gradually embracing your views of criminal treatment. . . . On looking about this state, I find that our two Lunatic Asylums and two out of three State Prisons, are now conducted, or are about to be, by the light of the new philosophy, and chiefly as it has been expounded by yourself." [5] At the same time from Boston came another comment on Sing Sing, "in which a very great reform has been introduced within three years, the law of love." [6]

The *American Phrenological Journal* hailed Sing Sing as a

4. Blake McKelvey, *American Prisons* (Chicago, 1936), p. 27.
5. *Phrenological Journal, 19* (1846), 198–9.
6. *Ibid.,* p. 199.

"phrenologically conducted institution," [7] while the New York *Observer,* a religious publication, complained that "the Sing Sing prison is witnessing a trial of your phrenology's tinkering, and the results you can chronicle in due time." [8] The *American Phrenological Journal* also ran articles on "the Law of Love," attacks on flogging and capital punishment, instances of the application of the new light on prison reform, and appreciation of judges and wardens who had followed its precepts. This was one of Fowlers and Wells' abiding interests, and as late as 1879 Linda Gilbert, the philanthropist who established libraries in prisons, was requesting her friend Professor Nelson Sizer to attend the next meeting of her group and examine heads.

Both the aforementioned commentators on the reforms introduced into Sing Sing remarked upon Mrs. Eliza Farnham, superintendent of the female department and "controlling spirit of the entire establishment." She contributed an enthusiastic preface and explanatory notes to the American edition of *Rationale of Crime and Its Appropriate Treatment,* by Marmaduke B. Sampson, an English phrenologist and London correspondent of the *American Phrenological Journal* (for this book Lorenzo N. Fowler selected the illustrations). She used to lecture to her charges from *The Constitution of Man,* as well as from Andrew Combe's *Physiology,* and make them study the former; in her notes to *Rationale of Crime* she described how she read it aloud, "placing it in the hands of our most intelligent convicts for private study," and added: "I know nothing more encouraging in the treatment of criminals, than the excellent effect which flows from imparting to them a knowledge of the peculiar constitution of their own mind. As soon as the source of their evil desires is brought clearly within their comprehension, all mystery, doubt and uncertainty are cleared away." [9] When a writer for the *American Journal of Insanity* asked if her success in the reform of criminals had been guided by the phrenological laws of the relations between mental

7. *American Phrenological Journal, 9* (1847), 133.
8. *Ibid.*
9. Marmaduke B. Sampson, *Rationale of Crime and Its Appropriate Treatment* (New York, 1846), p. 66 n.

manifestation and physical development, her answer was *"emphatically,* yes. A knowledge and adherence to those laws have been the foundation of whatever success has attended my efforts." [10] She was a well-known personage in her own field, and Charles Sumner referred to her in speaking of the experiments at Sing Sing as a person "whom we cannot name without a tribute of admiration." [11]

Together with William Henry Channing, yet another believer in the new dispensation, Sumner and his two associates, Horace Mann and Samuel Gridley Howe, were moving spirits in the Boston Prison Discipline Society, which published the *Prison Discipline Journal,* and in the New York Prison Association. In the 1840's Howe was sent to Europe to survey the prisons, schools, and asylums there; in his report is indicated at least one of the sources of his ideas:

> The doctrine of retributive justice is rapidly passing away, and with it will pass away, I hope, every kind of punishment that has not the reformation of the criminal in view. One of the first effects of this will be, I am sure, the decrease in the length of sentence and the adoption of some means by which the duration and severity of imprisonment may in all cases be modified by the conduct and character of the prisoners. What we want now—what no system I know of offers—is the means of training the prisoner's moral sentiments and his power of self-government by actual exercise.[12]

The Boston Prison Discipline Society broke apart in an open fight when Louis Dwight, its secretary, became infatuated with the congregate system of the Auburn Penitentiary, while Mann, Howe, and Sumner were more impressed with the moral virtues of the Pennsylvania solitary system. But Dwight overrode all opposition and in the Society's Eighteenth Report condemned the solitary system and quoted George Combe's and Charles Dickens' unfavorable opinions of it to bolster his own preference. This produced open mutiny by the insurgent trio, as expressed in the

10. *American Journal of Insanity, 2* (1845–46), 179.
11. *Christian Examiner, 40* (1846), 136.
12. Quoted in McKelvey, *American Prisons,* p. 28.

Report of a Minority of the Special Committee of the Boston Prison Discipline Society (Boston, 1846), which pointed out that Combe had been quoted out of context and that he really preferred the solitary system, as did they.

Probably the best known work of this period on criminal law was the proposed criminal code for the State of Louisiana by Edward Livingston, Andrew Jackson's Secretary of State and Minister to France; although it was never adopted, it was widely publicized and became famous throughout the United States and Europe. Like George Combe, Livingston advanced the theory that there were certain classes of incorrigible criminals who could be detected by phrenological examination; his code further resembled Combe's ideal system by providing for labor in solitude with congregate labor and human companionship as a reward for good conduct.[13] The phrenologists enthusiastically returned the compliment by hailing Livingston's recommendations as "a position much nearer that which is recognized by a sound philosophy of man . . . novel but eminently philosophical . . . ingenious as it is benevolent."

The parallelism and similarity of phrenological ideas to reform penology in general are obvious; however, that the debt is considerable is evidenced by the bitter criticism of conservatives, who identify the source of these new experiments. For example, the "Editor's Table" of *Harper's Magazine* burst forth in 1852:

> Its [phrenology's] aim is wholly to unspiritualize what has hitherto been called sin or crime. . . . Thus its features lose much of their intolerable hideousness. This undoubtedly is the great secret of the ready reception of phrenology, and phrenological works, in our penitentiaries and State prisons. Prison reformers maintain that Combe and Spurzheim produce repentance and reformation more than the Bible and direct preaching of Gospel. Phrenology locates crime in the brain

13. Edward Livingston, *Introductory Report to the Code of Reform and Prison Discipline*, pp. 32–5, and *Code of Reform and Prison Discipline*, pp. 20–2, both in his *A System of Penal Law for the United States of America* . . . (Washington, 1828); McKelvey, *American Prisons*, pp. 26–7.

. . . a physiological malady, cured by dietetic regimen, treated in hospitals and asylums, soothed into repentance with music, and flowers, and fetes, instead of whips and prisons and gallows.[14]

14. *Harpers' Magazine, 6* (1852–53), 126.

Chapter 9. Phrenology and Health

A new and more auspicious era . . . *The Constitution of Man* printed for the school . . . sickness a crime, death the penalty for violation of the laws of life . . . a new catalogue of criminal offences . . . sickness, improper diet, neglect of exercise, ill-assorted matches, and above all, deficiencies of brain in the right parts of the heads of our children, will be ranked with felony and misprision or treason.

New York Review, 1837

ACCORDING to the teachings of this new psychology, sanity and even virtue itself are dependent upon the normal functioning of the brain. But the brain is intimately related to the body—*mens sana* and *corpore sano* are virtually synonymous terms—and therefore the body as well as the soul should receive careful attention; if physical health is essential to efficiency and happiness, food and clothing are moral factors, as are sermons and schools. For these reasons the phrenologists with a fair amount of consistency could enter into the only apparently irrelevant crusade for health reform, and at times when they spoke of education, it was really physical education they meant.

Spurzheim took particular notice of the problem of American health and in his lectures tried to arouse interest in the problem of physical education; "in no country which he had visited, had he seen the women look so pale, languid, and feeble, as in this, and he attributed it to the small amount of exercise they took." [1] Dr. Amariah Brigham, in his many books forever blaming the ubiquitous American debility for the prevalence of insanity, thought

1. *Boston Medical and Surgical Journal,* quoted in *Annals of Education,* 6 (1836), 100.

Spurzheim's "visit will be productive of great good, by directing the attention of the public to the immense importance of physical education; a branch of education, the almost entire neglect of which, in this country, threatens dangerous and lasting consequences. . . . in a letter . . . he remarks upon the uncommon mental activity of the people of this country, and expresses his belief that the science which he taught would do great good here."[2]

After Spurzheim's untimely end, the torch in this particular field was caught up by Dr. William Grigg, who kept Spurzheim's 57-ounce brain in a glass vase in his office at the Boston Atheneum and used to deliver eulogies of the great man at the lyceums; he lectured against woman's fashions and to carry forward his system, "warmly approved by Spurzheim," projected a Callisthenium "with influential backing." The Boston Phrenological Society was soon issuing stern appraisals of the Boston juvenile schools, especially their lack of ventilation or playground facilities. Dr. Charles Caldwell, too, added his own brand of vigorously phrased assistance with *Thoughts on Physical Education*.

In this as in other notes of the phrenological gamut, George Combe's was the most eloquent and influential voice. Always his last lecture repeated the leitmotiv of the whole series:

> Again, phrenology shows us that, to improve the human mind, we must begin by improving the condition of the brain; and that, to attain success in this object, all moral, religious, and intellectual teaching must be conducted in harmony with the laws of physiology.[3]

To dramatize and reify his principles, as mentioned above, he directed the windows to be thrown open at the midpoint of his two-hour address and, to the horror of his audiences, the "deleterious" night air let in, recording his satisfaction when the skeptics found it refreshing. He did not hesitate to criticize the health and physical appearance of American womanhood—a suggestion of invalidism was fashionable during the "sentimental years"—and

2. Capen, *Reminiscences*, p. 131.
3. Combe, *Notes, 3,* 428–9.

for his pains a letter to a Philadelphia editor reproved him for offending the "national sense of propriety." His book about his American travels is filled with examples of what seemed to him wanton valetudinarianism; as his relative Fanny Kemble predicted, his account did "full justice to the perpetual infraction of his ever-present and sacred rules of life, by the people of the United States." [4] His lectures, his admirers told him, were responsible for not merely new school buildings in Boston but the fact that they were well-lighted and ventilated.

It is difficult to exaggerate the quasi-religious significance physiological law assumed in the true phrenologist's eyes. Dr. Andrew Combe, famous for his works on anatomy and digestion, thought he had "sinned" when afflicted by a toothache and said of his own writings: "The unvarying tendency of my mind is to regard the whole laws of the animal economy and of the universe as the direct dictates of the Deity; and in urging compliance with them, it is with the earnestness and deference due to a Divine command that I do it." [5] It is significant that both the Combes, like Horace Mann, were troubled with bad health in their youth, and the subject attained a mystic importance in their eyes. Horace Mann once said a dyspeptic stomach was "an abomination in the sight of God," [6] while Henry Ward Beecher felt that the secret of his success was that a phrenologist pronounced him "a splendid animal." [7] George Combe visited the manufacturer Abbot Lawrence, one of his partisans, just before Lawrence left for Congress in 1839, and found him in horror at the prospect of "the bad air in the chambers at Washington." [8]

The appeal for physical culture by the brothers Combe might have been deep and sincere, but it required the peculiar talents of the brothers Fowler really to popularize it. Similarities and differences between the two schools may be seen from this Fowler

4. Kemble, *Records of Later Life*, p. 167.
5. George Combe, *The Life and Correspondence of Andrew Combe* (Philadelphia, 1850), pp. 302–3.
6. *American Phrenological Journal*, 25 (1857), 33.
7. *Ibid.*, 27 (1858), 92.
8. Combe, *Notes*, 3, 174.

editorial of the 1850's: "On, ye Christians, and Christian ministers of every name and denomination! whom your Divine Master has pronounced to be the salt of the earth; in the name of science; in the name of all that is valuable in your holy religion; and in behalf of the present as well as the generation to come, I adjure you to wake up to this subject! Look well to the welfare of your *bodies,* if you would promote the welfare of your minds." [9] The Fowlers wrote books upon health and physical development, and always the practical side, how to attain those goals. A whole department of the *American Phrenological Journal* was devoted to physiology, as were several in the Fowlers' lecture series. Sometimes the new phrenological societies they sponsored had "physiological" in their titles too.

At the same time the Fowlers locked arms with other reformers of the same stamp and embraced a whole series of health reforms of every description. The *Journal* was adamant against the use of tobacco, tea, and coffee in any form. Samuel R. Wells was one of the moving spirits in the formation of the American Vegetarian Society. Sylvester Graham lectured at the Fowlers and Wells auditorium, Clinton Hall, and the *Journal* heartily recommended his brown bread, which the "senior editor lives almost exclusively on," [10] as well as his fresh fruits, cold showers, and cheerfulness at meals. Correct clothing was obviously important, and on the magazine's Index were tightly laced shoes and belts; the latter, it was said, affected the mind by cramping the organs, thereby injuring the Vital Temperament and making the Mental Temperament predominate.

The strictures concerning physical health and dress were addressed especially to American womanhood. Both Spurzheim and Combe commented upon the poor physical appearance and frailty of "the weaker sex" and what was worse, the almost deliberate insistence upon this frailty; yet the demands of fashion and the extreme modesty and prudery of contemporary mores seemingly forbade even the discussion of these subjects, let alone rectification. Into this forbidden territory, then, the Fowlers charged with-

9. *American Phrenological Journal,* 25 (1857), 33.
10. *Ibid., 18* (1853), 137.

out fear—and without research. Orson Fowler wrote numerous articles on the Evils of Tight Lacing; corsets were his particular abomination, and he suggested as a motto "natural waists or no wives." The *Journal* gave emphatic support to the costume originated by Mrs. Lydia Fowler's friend, Mrs. Amelia Bloomer. This ensemble, distinguished by long knickers, was "not Turkish, nor Persian, but American, suggested by the wants, and produced by the skill of the women of our own land." [11] Mrs. Lydia Fowler, along with her colleagues, Mary Gove Nichols and Mrs. E. Oakes Smith, contributed to female emancipation by lecturing to closed audiences on the forbidden subjects of female anatomy and feminine diseases, popular topics in the publishing list of Fowlers and Wells.

With their sure instinct for reform, controversy, and profit, the Fowlers could hardly have avoided the perpetually fascinating subject of sex. In 1845 Orson Fowler was including in his course of lectures separate addresses, first to male audiences and then to females, on "the facts of life," and after one such episode at Haverhill, Pennsylvania, was denounced by a clergyman for daring to speak on such forbidden topics. Like Freudianism, phrenology cast a new light on the subject of matrimony, which the Fowler group hastened to delineate in a spate of books: Orson's *Love and Parentage*, *Fowler on Matrimony*, and *Amativeness or Evils and Remedies of Excessive and Perverted Sexuality*, Lorenzo's *Marriage, Its History and Ceremonies*, and Nelson Sizer's *Thoughts on Domestic Life* and *Cupid's Eyes Opened and Mirror of Matrimony*. Despite their portentous titles and the hundreds of thousands of copies sold, these were not yet up to our own "plain wrapper" trade; their collective message is epitomized by the subtitle of Sizer's *Domestic Life*, "Marriage vindicated and free love exposed," and all are distinguished by extreme sentimentality.

Nevertheless, underlying this commercialism was a sincere belief in the need for reform. Thomas Low Nichols and Mary Gove Nichols, free spirits crusading for feminine freedoms, including sexual, were Fowlers and Wells authors as well as supporters of phrenology, and so was R. T. Trall, a pioneer in birth control:

11. *Ibid.*, *14* (1851), 45.

among their publications was Trall's *Uterine Diseases*, with fifty-three colored engravings. Late in his career Orson Fowler published *Sexual Science*, as graphic in its description as it was weird in its theory. The Fowlers were apparently regarded as authorities on the topic, to judge from a letter of William Henry Channing to Mrs. Charlotte Fowler Wells, which asks a great deal of information "from the experience of your office" [12] on the extent of licentiousness (with New York statistics) and remedies for it.

The taste for candy, cucumbers, coffee, and tea were symptoms of depraved appetites, but they were minor vices compared to that major sin, hard liquor. In a hard-drinking age the phrenologists en masse enlisted in the crusade for temperance. Drinking they looked upon not from the conventional spiritual point of view but, to quote Dr. Charles Caldwell, "as a form of mental derangement." It was a physical disease, a form of insanity, and Dr. Samuel B. Woodward proposed asylums for inebriates as well as lunatics. George Combe devoted a great deal of anxious attention and conversation to the problem of American drinking, and his *Notes on the United States* is the source of the familiar "striped pig" anecdote—a device to avoid the Sunday prohibition laws of Massachusetts.[13] The *American Phrenological Journal* probably attracted more attention than Combe in its unremitting opposition to alcohol: typical was its unsympathetic reaction to the tragic explosion aboard the battleship *Princeton* which killed the Secretary of State: "The bursting of that great gun on board the *Princeton* was preceded by the bursting of several bottles of champagne. . . . he that useth the sword shall perish by the sword." [14] With his motto "Natural waists or no wives," Orson Fowler used to bracket "Total abstinence or no husbands," and on his lecture tours it was his custom to speak at Sunday evening prayer services (without charge) on the evils of drink. Besides causing most of the world's woes, he declaimed, it inflamed the animal propensities (at the base

12. William Henry Channing to Charlotte Fowler Wells, September 21, 1851, Fowler-Wells Papers, Cornell University.

13. E.g. quoted in Allan Nevins, *Ordeal of the Union* (2 vols. New York, 1947), *1*, 127 n.

14. *American Phrenological Journal, 6* (1844), 80.

of the skull) rather than the (literally) higher moral faculties; the published version of this lecture the *Boston Medical and Surgical Journal* called "an ingenious contribution to the cause of temperance. . . . it may touch a string that no other argument has reached." [15]

Fowlers and Wells placed their press at the service of this crusade, printing and delivering at cost for mass distribution to the Temperance Societies copies of the Maine Liquor Law and pamphlets by Horace Mann, Horace Greeley, and others of their authors, including a series known as the "Whole World Temperance Tracts." The consonance between phrenology and temperance was indicated by the joint meetings of the Washington Phrenological and Temperance Societies; and that they were moving toward not temperance but prohibition was made clear by the Fowlers and Wells appeal: "KILL THIS BLACK TIGER, ye voting freemen!" [16]

The value of water was not just that it was a substitute for alcohol but that it had remarkable curative properties and therefore was a moral agent too. This discovery was made about 1829 by a Silesian peasant named Vincent Priesnitz, who cured his broken ribs by cold water and went on from there to a complete therapy of internal draughts of varying dimensions, and a great variety of external applications—showers, wet sheets, sitz baths, and enemas. This regimen filtered into the United States in the 1840's, not only as a guarantee of good health but as a cure for virtually any disease. Soon its practitioners flourished and their establishments, indoors and out, mushroomed all over the East, catering to the "forward thinking." Soon too appeared the inevitable, the *Water Cure Journal,* conducted by Dr. Joel Shew and hailed by the *American Phrenological Journal,* whose hospitable columns phrenologized Herr Priesnitz and recorded the wonder works of this new treatment. In 1848, after the *Water Cure Journal* had fallen into financial difficulties and during a hiatus in publication, came the announcement that "the editor having tried it," Fowlers and Wells was taking it over. For it the firm prescribed

15. Quoted in Orson S. Fowler, *A Lecture on Temperance Considered Physiologically and Phrenologically* (New York, 1851), p. ii.
16. *Ibid.,* p. 12.

the same treatment it had previously given the *American Phreno-logical Journal:* adding the title "and Herald of Reforms" and administering the Fowler brand of journalism and a generous dose of phrenology. Soon the *Water Cure Journal* had a circulation of 10,000 a month.

After and before: the water cure

Fowlers and Wells published many books on hydropathy, and it wasn't long before this new church had its own seminary, the American Hydropathic Institute, run by those tireless reformers, Thomas Low Nichols and Mary Gove Nichols, to staff the many water cure establishments dotting the American countryside. When the Nichols' team transferred its operations to Cincinnati in 1854, the Institute was succeeded by R. T. Trall's New York Hydropathic and Physiological School, with fifty students and a full curriculum and faculty, including Lorenzo Fowler.

All these reforms and reformers, by a process of syncretism, seemed to get mixed in together. The phrenologists were reformers almost by definition, and apparently the vast majority of the reformers were sympathetic to phrenology. Phrenology, Graham crackers, dress reform, fresh air, sex hygiene, temperance, the water cure, and sunlight formed a united front with vibrant moral overtones. When Amelia Bloomer visited New York, she was the guest of Lorenzo ("the great phrenologist") and Lydia Fowler, at whose home she met Horace Greeley; she naively recorded in her diary that she attended with her hosts a great banquet (vegetarian), at which, "it was said by the newspapers of the day, were gathered all the reformers of every description." [17] The Bloomers stayed with the Fowlers also on February 7, 1853, the night of the Woman's Grand Temperance Demonstration at Metropolitan Hall. Mrs. Fowler was chosen President and harangued the large and fashionable gathering, the first in New York in which women spoke from the public platform; she did not, however, wear the tunic and bloomers of her more strong-minded sisters.

The phrenological bush was rooted in the soil of reform, and, as we have seen, some of its branches were far removed from the seed sown by Franz Joseph Gall less than a half-century before. But in 1848 even the hardened readers of the *American Phrenological Journal* must have considered the connection between their favorite science and this, their favorite reading material, somewhat tenuous. It all began with a conventional article in the January, 1848, issue upon the phrenological faculty of Constructiveness, which "gives an excellent practical idea of the best mode of constructing things. . . . How beautiful, how necessary, the possession of this faculty of man; and how innumerable and great the good it confers." [18] In the next issue followed an account of the phrenological faculty of Inhabitativeness, headed "Home! sweet, sweet home! there's no place like home." In the ensuing analysis Orson Fowler assured his readers that the desire to possess a home, however modest, was normal and admirable, even though when this organ was over-developed it resulted in the Swiss malady called "home-sickness"; a man should provide the best home he can, but in contrast to the "try-to-be extra exquisite monument" of "immatured tastes," "the more powerful a man's intellect, and the better balanced his mind, the more perfect mansion will he construct." [19]

17. D. C. Bloomer, *Life and Writings of Amelia Bloomer* (Boston, 1895), p. 135.
18. *American Phrenological Journal, 10* (1848), 22–3.
19. *Ibid.,* pp. 60–1.

In brief, what had happened was that although Lorenzo Fowler was established at a handsome residence on East Broadway, Orson Fowler and his wife still were without a permanent residence, due to the peripatetic nature of his calling. Having amassed a considerable personal fortune, he purchased some land near Fishkill on the Hudson, and his versatile mind, unimpressed by tradition, imbued with science, and conversant with American architecture north, south, east, and west, set itself the problem of devising a home. The result, as might be expected, was far from conventional. His plans, which appeared in the March, 1848, issue of the *American Phrenological Journal,* read like something from 20th-century functionalism. Fowler argued, apparently without plagiarism, that the spherical form enclosed the most space for the least amount of wall; since that was impractical in architecture, he advocated an octagonal structure (the closest approximation to a sphere in building) as the most efficient and ideal home.[20]

Two years later he made a tour of the West and at Jaynesville, Wisconsin, viewed the wonders of a building called "Goodrich's Folly," which was made of lime, sand, and small stones—a material that looked like concrete and was called "grout" or "gravel wall." This was cheap, impervious, and avoided the problem of costly construction of angles in wood, brick, or stone.

These two innovations, then, were the foundations of his architectural credo, upon which he built his own home, constructed between 1850 and 1854, with frequent lapses while he went off on another tour to gain enough money to continue the building. The glories of this pleasure dome were finally there for all to see; and for those too remote to journey to Fishkill there was the inevitable Fowler book, *A Home for All, or the Gravel Wall and Octagon Mode of Building.* Even for an unusual man, it was a most un-

20. The octagon form, of course, goes back to classical architecture and was used by 18th- and 19th-century British and American architects, among them Thomas Jefferson. Fowler claimed priority only in applying it to domestic residences and in using it for practical and utilitarian reasons of economy and efficiency rather than aesthetic and formal reasons. An exact modern analogy is R. Buckminster Fuller's "Dymaxion House," which is spherical and built of aluminum, plexiglass, and plywood. See *Life,* April 1, 1946, pp. 73–6.

usual home. Its main entrance was at the basement level, from whose kitchens one passed up the central stairwell some seventy feet high to the fourth floor veranda, which was lighted by a

A "home for all": Fowler's octagon

cupola of Crystal Palace glass. The first floor consisted of four large rooms—dining room, parlor, drawing room, and amusement room. When opened together by folding doors, they formed a single area of about 3,000 square feet. The two upper stories consisted of bedrooms, and all floors were surrounded by spacious continuous balconies. Always intoxicated by technology, Fowler added such innovations as a hot-air furnace, indoor water closets, speaking tubes, and a dumb-waiter, as well as such novelties as "a gymnastic room for females" and a dancing room. The completed structure contained over sixty-five rooms and was eventually sold for $150,-000, which would seem to belie its inevitable title of "Fowler's Folly."

Orson held receptions, lectures, and summer courses at his new home; hundreds came to consult the great professor, perhaps as many more to see his magnificent contribution to architecture. All through the country rugged individualists in general, and phrenologists in particular, began to build octagonal homes; there are many still standing today, especially in the Hudson River Valley.

Fowler's primary purpose in publishing his book and exhibiting his home was not publicity or profit; his watchword, like his generation's, was reform, and he would have been the first to admit that a house with almost a hundred rooms was hardly "a home for all." He meant, so read the first words of his book, "to cheapen and improve human homes, and especially to bring comfortable dwellings within the reach of the poorer classes," and his solution lay in the universal efficacy of the plain, semistandardized, and pseudo-scientific octagon. His credo, like Louis Sullivan's, was "form follows function," and by using the reasoning of science and breaking the cake of custom, he felt that good housing could be brought to the common man. His goal was to bring the progress to architecture that was evident in mental science, diet, physical hygiene, and all other phases of human life: "Is no *radical* improvement possible there, when there is so much in all other matters?" 21

21. Orson S. Fowler, *A Home for All, or the Gravel Wall and Octagon Mode of Building* (2d ed. New York, 1854), p. iv. This work went through at least seven editions in nine years and was widely copied and quoted in contemporary builders' books.

Chapter 10. Phrenology and Literature

But lo! the craniologist appears, and a blaze of intelligence illumines the page of history.

Ariel, 1832

THOSE who had erected a mighty inverted pyramid upon the anatomical observations of Gall soon claimed for it a philosophy of universal scope. Like a searchlight, they thought, it could pierce the gloom of the past as well as illuminate the future, could be turned upon creations of the imagination as well as the physical world, could comprehend art as well as science; phrenology could be used not just to reform but to understand, to *know*.

One of the protean forms of this new doctrine was a system of human psychology which purported to explain how men were constituted and how and why they acted. Therefore, it soon occurred to the literati of the phrenological societies that one could phrenologize the dead as well as the living; like the Freudian critics of our own day, they began to analyze the characters of literature, and soon among the lists of papers read at the phrenological societies and the tables of contents of the phrenological periodicals were analyses of such figures as Iago and Hamlet. So essential was this as a means to the understanding of famous men, as opposed to the mere facts of their lives and actions, that James Parton appended an essay by Lorenzo Niles Fowler to his biography of Aaron Burr and commended it to his readers.

Phrenology could come to the aid of artist as well as reader. The painter and sculptor, in representing great men of the past or symbolic creations, knew from their subjects' characters what they must have looked like, what they *had* to look like—art, in other words, should imitate life. George Combe could with consistency criticize Raphael's School of Athens—Cicero and Demosthenes, he said, should have had larger organs of language.

But it was in the quick brush strokes of imaginative fiction that the phrenological coloring is most apparent. Phrenology had spread through the stream of American thought, and 19th-century literature is filled with phrenological interpretations and expressions; for, as *Harper's* bitterly complained, the new science had infected thought at its very source, through language. Sometimes references to it were simply humorous—like Melville's involved discussion of the phrenology of the whale in *Moby Dick*—or metaphoric—as when Thoreau said the American "Odd Fellow" was distinguished by a lack of intellect and a development of the "organ of gregariousness." [1] Such examples, of course, indicate no more than general acquaintance with phrenological ideas and terminology, but at the same time they were a means of widening that current.

Other authors, assuming that the general principles of phrenology were readily understood by readers, endowed their principals with the appropriate cranial topographies. In Caroline Lee Hentz's *Eoline,* for instance, the school teacher's choice of a profession is vindicated by a consultation, for "her organs of Self-Esteem and Firmness were, indeed, most wonderfully developed" while her "physiology indicates a predominance of the nervous temperament." [2] In the novel of the "sentimental years" more important than beauty or dress, sometimes it appears, is the shape of the head. Xanthine's lovely hair, in C. Burdett's *Blonde and Brunette,* covered "a soft antique fulness in the region of ideality," [3] while an examination of the skull of the hero of Anna Corat Mowatt's *The Fortune Hunter* "would have been a delight to Spurzheim. Nature's own hand clustered the dark curls around his broad high forehead." [4] The silhouette of Dr. Hopkins, in Harriet Beecher

1. "Essay on Civil Disobedience."
2. C. L. Hentz, *Eoline* (Philadelphia, 1869), p. 137. All the examples in this paragraph are cited in Herbert R. Brown, *The Sentimental Novel in America, 1789–1860,* Durham, N.C., 1940.
3. Charles Burdett, *Blonde and Brunette* (New York, 1858), p. 25.
4. Anna Corat Mowatt, *The Fortune Hunter* (Philadelphia, 1854), p. 23.

Stowe's *The Minister's Wooing,* was delineated with scientific precision, "the squareness of ideality giving marked effect to its outline." [5] Minor stereotyped characters—speculators, ministers, servants—were fitted with the "bump" appropriate to their single dimension.

This does not mean, of course, that American novelists were the only authors who used phrenological terms and interpretations in their works, or that they were the only authors who were habituating the American reading public to the thought and expression of the new science. The novels of Bulwer-Lytton, Charlotte Brontë, and George Eliot, to mention only a few English writers popular with the American reading public, furnish abundant illustrations of phrenological terms and concepts.

Few American authors were more in tune with the *Zeitgeist* than Edgar Allan Poe, and this brought him within the orbit of the new science. There is no literary evidence of any concern with the subject before 1836, but in March of that year, as an editor of the *Southern Literary Messenger,* he reviewed rhapsodically the American edition of Mrs. L. Miles' *Phrenology, and the Moral Influence of Phrenology:* "Phrenology is no longer to be laughed at. It is no longer laughed at by men of common understanding. It has assumed the majesty of a science, and, as a science ranks among the most important which can engage the attention of thinking beings —this too, whether we consider it merely as an object of speculative inquiry, or as involving consequences of the highest practical magnitude." [6] Soon he was criticizing Robert Walsh's *Didactics: Social, Literary, and Political* because it was hostile to phrenology.

Poe regretted that he should have "to see the energies of a scholar and an editor . . . so wickedly employed as in any attempt to throw ridicule upon a question . . . whose merits he has never examined, and of whose very nature, history, and assumption, he

5. Harriet Beecher Stowe, *The Minister's Wooing* (New York, 1886; 1st ed. 1859), p. 92.

6. *Southern Literary Messenger,* 2 (1835–36), 286. My discussion of Poe and Whitman is based on an interview with Professor Edward Hungerford and his articles in *American Literature,* 2 (1930–31), 209–31, 350–84.

is most evidently ignorant." [7] Thereafter he seems to have delved into the new philosophy, probably attending George Combe's lectures in Philadelphia in 1839, and his references to it were frequent and its influence upon him profound.

Just a month after Poe had reviewed Mrs. Miles, his regular contribution to the *Southern Literary Messenger* was on the nature of poetry, which he set out to analyze intellectually. The phrenologists, he said, had divided the mind into basic, primitive faculties, among which was Ideality, "the sense of the beautiful, of the sublime, and of the mystical." Using the vocabulary of this new approach, he went on to build a theory of literary criticism; poetry was the practical result of this faculty of Ideality. And that was the trouble with Joseph Rodman Drake's "The Culprit Fay," which its critics had failed to perceive; Drake was adept at the faculty of Comparison but he lacked Ideality.

Poe continued with this phrenological approach to artistic creation until the end of his brief career. It is ironical that he, a prime target for literary psychoanalysis today, should have turned its contemporary equivalent upon his own colleagues. In 1850 was published his series of sketches of the literary figures of New York City, and imbedded in each description was a quick cranial topography; in the case of William Cullen Bryant, for example, "the forehead is broad, with prominent organs of Ideality." [8]

As might be expected, Poe's fiction is filled with references to his favorite psychology. Most of them are of the same order as Harriet Beecher Stowe's, or his own humorous descriptions of his fellow authors; for example, both "The Imp of the Perverse" and "The Murders in the Rue Morgue" have as their introductions and springboards discussions of the phrenological analysis of human faculties. But while a knowledge of 19th-century psychiatry may increase our knowledge of what Poe meant, it hardly enhances our appreciation of him as a literary artist; in these instances his use of phrenology is essentially descriptive, like a modern au-

7. *The Complete Works of Edgar Allan Poe,* ed. James A. Harrison (17 vols. New York, 1902), *8,* 329.

8. Edgar Allan Poe, *The Literati* (New York, 1850), p. 188.

thor describing his characters as extroverts or with specific complexes.

Occasionally, however, it is necessary to comprehend thoroughly the connotation of his allusions in order to understand the subtlety of his writing. In "The Fall of the House of Usher," for example,

The "Nervous" temperament: Edgar Allan Poe

Roderick Usher has an "inordinate expansion above the regions of the temple," [9] indicating to the cognoscenti that he was extraordinarily endowed with the organ of Ideality and thus able to dash off such verses as "The Haunted Palace." Furthermore, the "ghastly pallor of the skin . . . miraculous lustre of the eye . . . wild gossamer texture" [10] of the hair indicated (to amateur psychologists) that this is an extreme example of the "Nervous" temperament. It was only Poe's first readers who fully understood the impact of the gloomy scene and these grisly events upon the peculiar temper-

9. Poe, *Works, 3,* 279.
10. *Ibid.*

ament of Roderick Usher and thus could completely appreciate his special tragedy and the full subtlety of the characterization.

While a knowledge of phrenology might change slightly our conception of Poe, it hardly changed Poe's conception of himself. The same cannot be said of another author-journalist-reviewer, Walt Whitman. Like Poe, Whitman apparently had his first contact with the new doctrine when he reviewed one of its books; the following appeared in the November 16, 1846, issue of the *Brooklyn Daily Eagle* and is in much the same vein as Poe's in the *Southern Literary Messenger* a decade earlier:

> Breasting the waves of detraction as a ship dashes sea-waves, phrenology, it must now be confessed by all men who have open eyes, has at last gained a position, and a firm one, among the sciences. It seems useless to deny this—and the only difference is as to the laying down of the dividing lines, and how distinctly and authoritatively they can be marked. Perhaps no philosophic revolutionisers ever were attacked with more virulence—struck with more sinewy arms, or greater perseverance —than Gall, Spurzheim, and the other early phrenologists. The great organs of taste, and criticism, and judges of literary merit, in the British Islands, came "down" upon them as tempests come down on the oak. But the phrenologists withstood the storm and have gained the victory.

In his old age Whitman still remembered the Phrenological Cabinet as one of the showplaces of New York and one of his favorite places to visit. In July, 1849, he had himself phrenologized by Lorenzo Fowler, and the resultant diagnosis was impressive indeed, as might be expected from his splendid head. Walt Whitman, according to the findings of "science," was a marvelously developed man, being deficient in no aspect of the human mind and liberally endowed in most; his faults, such as they were, came from an overabundance of sheer humanity: "leading traits of character appear to be Friendship, Sympathy, Sublimity and Self-Esteem, and markedly among his combinations the dangerous faults of Indolence, a tendency to the pleasure of Voluptuousness and Alimentativeness, and a certain swing of animal will, too unmindful, probably, of the conviction of others." [11]

Whitman never quite got over it. He kept the chart until the end of his life and had it published five times. Now he began to study phrenology and ever after viewed human nature through the special analytical lenses of this psychology. The experience changed his whole conception of himself and provided him with a scientific interpretation of human character on which to base his poetry. He became the prophet of American democracy, because, according to his transcendental theory of poetry, all life and human nature were implicit in himself.

Consequently, when he came to write *Leaves of Grass,* in its preface he told his readers that "large hope and comparison . . . large alimentativeness and destructiveness and causality [precisely the organs he himself excelled in] . . . are called up of the float of the brain of the world to be parts of the greatest poet. . . . the atomist chemist astronomer geologist phrenologist spiritualist mathematician historian are not poets, but they are the lawgivers of poets and their construction underlies the structure of every perfect poem. . . . in the beauty of poems are the tuft and final applause of science." The poems themselves exemplify the teachings of phrenology in their general spirit of individualism, optimism, and worship of the body, and frequently even employ phrenological terminology. "A Song of Joys," for instance, is a catalogue of the pleasures of man, each of these pleasures derived from the exercise of one of the faculties of the brain as defined by the new psychology; it is quite apparent that it was written as a poetic description of the phrenological organs and was conceived with specific reference to a particular book, which he had probably acquired from Fowlers and Wells.

Whitman thus had a spiritual affiliation with the phrenologists; eventually it became a physical one too. The cheerful reformers of the Phrenological Cabinet were, consistently enough, admirers of *Leaves of Grass* and put the first edition of these experi-

11. This was bound into the 1855 edition of *Leaves of Grass* and is reprinted in Horace L. Traubel, Richard M. Bucke, and Thomas B. Harned, eds., *In Re Walt Whitman* (Philadelphia, 1893), p. 25 n.

mental verses on sale July 5, 1855. When the other booksellers handling it became disturbed over the initial reaction and dropped the book, Fowlers and Wells stayed with it and continued to promote it until 1858. Moreover, Lorenzo Fowler gave Whitman the opportunity every author dreams of, the chance to review his own book (anonymously): "He [Whitman] speaks of himself as sterile on the old myths, and all the customary themes of romantic and classical writers, but pregnant with the deductions of the geologist, the astronomer, the great antiquary, the chemist, the phrenologist, the spiritualist, the mathematician, and with the ideas and practice of American politics." [12] The next year Whitman became a staff writer for *Life Illustrated,* another Fowlers and Wells publication, and contributed a whole sheaf of signed articles, the collective tenor of which is indicated by the title of one series: "New York Dissected." But his association with and his debt to Fowlers and Wells were by no means his reason for reprinting his own phrenological chart with the late 1855 and 1856 editions of *Leaves of Grass:* he put his faith in that chart, for it proved his ability and his personality.

12. *American Phrenological Journal,* 22 (1855), 90.

Chapter 11. Phrenomagnetism

> We can easily imagine how unwilling many intelligent phrenologists will be, to see our favorite science connected, in any way, with the subject of living Magnetism. The former they believe to be true, of the latter they know nothing, except the stigma in which it has been involved by the ignorance of its friends, and the aspersions cast upon it by enemies who were unwilling to give this an equal chance with the claims of other branches of science. But it will certainly change the views of such believers in phrenology, when they come to find, as they will, sooner or later, that, without Magnetism, phrenology is no more than a body without a soul. For, what is the brain, or its various developments, without *life?*
>
> The *Magnet, 1842*

THE READERS of the *American Phrenological Journal* found twelve extra pages added to one of the issues of Volume *4,* in order to give complete coverage to some "indescribably beautiful and philosophical discoveries." [1] These "discoveries" were to prove of some importance to the later career of the new psychology, since they married it to (another) pseudoscience; in order to understand the resultant offspring, one must know something of its ancestry.

In 1836 a Frenchman living in this country, Charles Poyen, began lecturing through New England on the art of Anton Mesmer, which he had studied in his youth. Although mesmerism enjoyed no great vogue at first, after two or three years a delayed reflex occurred, and as Orestes Brownson wrote in his autobiographical novel *The Spirit Rapper,* "Animal Magnetism soon became the fashion, in the principal towns and villages of the Eastern and Middle States. Old men and women, young men and maidens,

1. *American Phrenological Journal, 4* (1842), 86.

boys and girls, of all classes and sizes, were engaged in studying the mesmeric phenomena, and mesmerizing or being mesmerized." [2] In the eyes of skeptics it was the experience of phrenology repeating itself: another Austrian pseudoscience introduced by foreign lecturers and perpetuated by Americans in search of profit who purveyed entertainment to the gullible. This was bitterly denied by the phrenologists, who claimed that while hypnotism was a sort of parlor game, their own doctrine was of demonstrable social utility and was a completely rational science.

In any case, the two movements went their separate (and sometimes competing) ways, hypnotism confined to the entertainment world and to the few "operators" who had tried it as an anesthetic, phrenology advancing, as we have seen, on different levels. Then in 1842 occurred the familiar sociological phenomenon of simultaneous discovery when several magnetizers—the priority is not clear, although the claimants several—successfully carried through a new experiment of placing their hands upon the separate mental (phrenological) organs of their "patients" during the "magnetic sleep" and thereby, it was asserted, inducing these faculties to exhibit their "appropriate language" in a "pure state." The results were described by one awed beholder, Robert Dale Owen, as follows:

> The organs giving playfulness and good humor, were excited; and the subject . . . bent forward, smiled, his arms relaxed, his embarrassment was gone, and his whole air was that of ease and mirthful sympathy. The effect was infectious; and the audience indulged in laughter, in which . . . he himself joined. Suddenly the operator raised his hand, and placed it on the organ of self-esteem. An enchanter's wand could not have produced a transformation more sudden and complete. Every expression of mirth or playfulness vanished at the touch; the body was thrown back even beyond the perpendicular; the chin elevated; the legs crossed consequentially; the relaxed arms drawn up, one hand placed on the breast, the other a-kimbo; and a side-long glance of the most supercilious con-

2. Orestes Brownson, *The Spirit Rapper* (Boston, 1854), p. 23.

tempt, cast on the audience, convulsed them with laughter.
The subject of their mirth, however, remained utterly un-
moved; not a muscle of the face relaxed; and the expression of
proud scorn seemed to harden on his countenance.[3]

This performance soon became a standard item in the repertoire of the itinerant hypnotist, and for it appeared another
neologism, "phrenomagnetism." A profound tremor went through
the world of phrenology, whether to disavow this unexpected offspring or to legitimize it. To affiliate with mesmerism would be to
enter into a liaison with "show business" and with a doctrine
which had no reputable supporters, had been condemned a half
century before by an eminent scientific committee—including
Benjamin Franklin—and had served no scientific or utilitarian
purpose. On the perilous voyage to respectability phrenology was
having enough trouble; one more stowaway might founder the
whole enterprise.

On the other hand, the phrenologists would lose all claim to
consistency or to scientific pretensions if they should deny a hearing to another approach to mental research, especially when to
any impartial mind it was apparent that whatever the explanation
for the remarkable results of the phrenomagnetists, deliberate de-
ception was not one.[4] What was more important, thus far phrenology had depended on three modes of proof, all acceptable
within the framework of early 19th-century science: arguments
from anatomy, pathology, and cranioscopy. None of these was completely satisfactory, as attested by the legions of dissenters, but
here was the possibility of incontestable evidence—as one enthusiastic Englishman put it who had witnessed the American experiments, of "irrefragable proof." [5]

In most cases the temptation, alluring as it might appear, was
not enough. George Combe, although he was willing to admit the

3. *Phreno-Magnet, 1* (London, 1843), 12–13.
4. The observation was soon made, without comprehension of its significance, that phrenomagnetism was not successful with subjects who had
never seen a phrenological chart.
5. Glasgow *Phrenological Almanac, 2* (1843), 52.

fact of mesmerism, rather perceptively asserted that phrenomagnetism was simply the operator imposing his will on the subject and
wryly observed that its partisans had large organs of "Wonder."
Among the elder and more intellectual advocates of Spurzheim,
only one espoused this new auxiliary, and that was the old defender
of lost causes, Charles Caldwell.

Orson Fowler was urged not to open the columns of the *American Phrenological Journal* to these discoveries, lest that open up a
second front of derision, but he bravely replied "with *consequences*
I have nothing to do, only with *truth.*" His motives, one feels, are
more exactly revealed by a few words from another editorial: "is
not this subject wonderful partly because it is *new?*" [6] The weather-
vane minds of the Fowlers and their group were peculiarly conditioned to the changing winds of reform, and soon the pages of the
Journal were overflowing with ecstatic accounts of discoveries
"most extraordinary and the most important to mankind," [7]
liberally punctuated with exclamation points. With hypnotism itself the Fowlers were not unfamiliar, since Orson said he suggested the *idea* of phrenomagnetism five years before and had recently "cured" a young lady of toothache, while Lorenzo had
magnetized a woman when she had a tumor removed. Soon an exhibition of phrenomagnetism was added to the repertoire of
Fowler lectures, but despite Orson's experience as both operator
and subject, he was obliged to refuse treating illnesses, "because
he is liable to *take on* the disease for which he magnetizes." [8] Further corners to this Pandora's box were the treatment of insanity
and the use of post-hypnotic suggestion, weaning alcoholics from
the bottle "for several weeks. . . . the time is not far off when the
power of casting out devils will be practiced." [9]

The fertile brains of Orson Fowler and his fellow spirits conceived new vistas for this novel technique. Not only would it serve
to check the hypotheses of Spurzheim—and it confirmed every
organ in every detail—but it also might be the means of discover-

6. *American Phrenological Journal, 4* (1842), 316, 187.
7. *Ibid., 5* (1843), 23.
8. *Ibid., 8* (1846), 126.
9. *Ibid., 4* (1842), 217.

ing new ones. By agitating minute subdivisions of the skull and careful observation of the consequent reflexes one could detect, they believed, subtle variations in the "appropriate language" of the organs, and this led to the conclusion that the original organs were not unitary but really "families," and that the faculties numbered not thirty-five but ninety-one; of course, this analysis became rather specialized, as when Philoprogenitiveness was resolved into Parental Love, Filial Love, and—the ultimate—Love of Pets. In this manner eighty-three separate organs were distinguished, renamed, and renumbered.

Thus phrenology found new confirmation and sighted new horizons, and the *American Phrenological Journal* acquired a new department. Along with this new stimulus the science recruited some unusual troops. La Roy Sunderland, a Methodist revivalist and radical abolitionist in continuous trouble with his presiding bishops, decided that his success in revivalism was due not to the power of the Methodist God but that of hypnotism, and he withdrew from the church. The Reverend Sunderland had been studying mesmerism, conducting experiments with his friends Orson Fowler and Dr. H. H. Sherwood (another Fowlers and Wells associate and reformer), and claimed to be the discoverer of phrenomagnetism. Now in imitation of his friend and his magazine, Sunderland became editor of a journal, the *Magnet,* to spearhead that movement; this new publication covered the fields of Physiology, Physiognomy, Phrenology, Pathogeny, Psychology, Magnetism, and (later) Cephology, Pathology, Neurology, Electricity, Galvanism, Light, Caloric, and Life. Despite this universal grasp, the *Magnet* expired after three troubled years, handing on the torch to the *American Phrenological Journal.* Sunderland continued for forty more years, however, and free spirit to the end, evolved a system he called "pathetism" and discovered 150 more phrenological organs.

Occasionally societies were formed to study the new science, for example the Phreno-magnetic Society of Cincinnati, which was organized in July, 1842, and consisted of some fifty members. Its purpose was to study the phenomena of magnetic sleep and induced somnambulism, and a typical meeting centered around such performances as these: "he commenced by exciting the organ of *Veneration*. His face instantly assumed a solemn and beautiful expression, whilst, in a subdued but sweet tone of voice, he exclaimed, 'Spare us,'—'He died for us.' . . . This was a powerful and beautiful manifestation." [10] Unfortunately its journal expired with Volume *1*, Number 1, and with it our knowledge of the organization's history.

One of the visiting scholars who appeared before the Cincinnati society was the fabulous Joseph Rodes Buchanan of Louisville, an itinerant lecturer on phrenology and its allied sciences throughout the South and Midwest. He heatedly denied the Reverend Sunderland's priority in discovering phrenomagnetic manipulation and came east to assert his preeminence; in some newspapers (on dull days) this controversy assumed the proportions of that between Peary and Cook some sixty-seven years later. Buchanan lectured in Boston first for six months and then moved upon New York, meaning, of course, Clinton Hall. In Boston a committee of eminent scientists and Brahmins, including Bowditches, Lowells, Everetts, and (for variety) Horace Mann, made a study of his experiments but cautiously refused to issue its report; the New York commission, which had on its roster William Cullen Bryant and J. Louis O'Sullivan, after extensive observation concluded that his views had "a rational, experimental foundation." [11] The *American Phrenological Journal* characteristically reported with enthusiasm Buchanan's transpositions of old organs and discovery of ninety-one new ones, but soon even that most open-minded of publications began to dash cold water on this fresh breeze from the west and found that "he is somewhat given to making *speculative inferences* . . . and to regard all the rest of phrenologists as novices." [12] Undoubtedly he *was* a rather difficult colleague and would later be described as "a man who loved humanity in general, who hated his neighbors, and who throughout his long life

10. *Journal of the Phreno-Magnetic Society of Cincinnati, 1* (1842), 2.
11. *United States Magazine and Democratic Review, 12* (1843), 81.
12. *American Phrenological Journal, 5* (1843), 37.

remained peculiarly gifted with self-confidence, expressed in his erect carriage, lifted head, and smile of infinite condescension." [13]

It was not due to Buchanan's character alone that the *American Phrenological Journal* reprinted his revelations only in brief (and the Edinburgh *Phrenological Journal* not at all). He had combined phrenology, animal magnetism, and medicine into a wonderfully incoherent system which he variously termed "neurology" or "sarcognomy." In brief, in his researches he had discovered that the principle of cerebral localization of function went further than the phrenologists themselves had imagined; now it developed that every organ of the body was directed by a separate region of the brain, with which it was intimately connected. Therefore by examining a brain (by means of the "nervaura," an invisible electrical nervous emanation) he could diagnose the health of the parts of the body, and by the same method could treat any particular organ by directing his hypnotic therapy to the appropriate region of the skull. These were only parts of the complicated and wondrous philosophy of Buchanan, embalmed in many stout volumes and a periodical of his own, the *Journal of Man*. He lived out fifty-five more years of disputation and, prodigy to the last, at the age of eighty-three wrote a collective biography of the early Christian Apostles, dictated to him "by the subjects themselves."

Another pioneer in science and tiller in this profitable field was Robert H. Collyer, who arrived in the United States in June, 1836. Although he had been a student and friend of Spurzheim in England, he by no means received the same welcome as George Combe. Everywhere were "unprincipled quacks" who took advantage of the interest Spurzheim had aroused, and when Collyer began lecturing in New York City, these "Yankee speculators" memorized his very words and style. After a long tour through the South and West, he returned to Peale's Museum in New York and (by his own account, the mordant *Lights and Shadows of American Life*) he too introduced phrenomagnetism to the American public; but a certain "L. R. S. [underland, promoter of the *Magnet*]" falsely claimed the invention: "Yankees are said to have the faculty of imitation in a remarkable degree." Now that Collyer had awak-

13. Ernest Sutherland Bates, "Joseph Rodes Buchanan," in *DAB*.

ened interest in the subject, "hundreds of ignorant mechanics, carpenters, painters, furriers, scavengers, barbers . . . not a few . . . broken down phrenologists" attempted a new career and then slandered and injured him "to *make money.*" [14]

According to Collyer the most unkindest cut of all was by an American who claimed to have the same name and to practice the same profession. In 1839 the second Collyer was graduated from the Medical College in Pittsfield, Massachusetts, and "converted to the mesmeric truth." [15] He too hit the sawdust trail, and like all the rest, "invented" phrenomagnetism as well as his own neologism, "psychography," and wrote a book. He seems to have been the archetype "Yankee" and butt for his namesake's fulminations, since by 1843 Orson Fowler, too, had denounced his immoralities and was calling upon his readers for affidavits concerning his crimes, defaults, and seductions.

A final example of this new school of philosophers was James Stanley Grimes, lawyer, professor, lecturer, and controversialist. He began by attacking the orthodox classification by Spurzheim of the phrenological organs and proposed dividing them into "ranges," with the intriguing names of ipseal, carniverous, herbiverous, rodenta, and so forth. Although supported by the Albany Phrenological Society,[16] his system was criticized by the *American Phrenological Journal.*[17] From this discipline and the new mesmerism Grimes went on to evolve "etherology," in which cosmic system he attacked Joseph Rodes Buchanan's "nervaura" but proposed in its place an occult fluid of his own—"etherium," an invisible substance responsible for the transmission of everything from electricity to hypnotism and the absence of which produced death. From this remarkable substance he advanced to new dis-

14. Collyer, *Lights and Shadows of American Life,* pp. 15–16, 34.

15. Robert H. Collyer, *Psychography, or, the Embodiment of Thought, with an Analysis of Phreno-Magnetism, "Neurology," and Mental Hallucination, including Rules to Govern and Produce the Magnetic States* (Philadelphia, 1843), p. 38.

16. Edward N. Horsford, *Report on the Phrenological Classification of J. Stanley Grimes, Adopted by the Albany Phrenological Society, Sept. 3, 1840,* Albany, 1840.

17. *American Phrenological Journal,* 2 (1839–40), 529–41.

coveries, in *Phreno-geology* (1851) and *Geonomy* (1858). Again like the rest of these new spirits, he lived to a ripe old age, departing these fields only in 1903 in his ninety-sixth year.

The usual criticism of phrenology had been that it was materialistic and mechanistic, reducing the mind to a machine and denying the spiritual world. But with the ally of hypnotism it seemed to be veering in another direction, toward spiritualism and the occult. According to a similar theory of Joseph Rodes Buchanan called "psychometry," a magnetizer, with the aid of an especially talented subject (and the "nervaura"), could diagnose the ills and read the character of a person who was not present or, for that matter, alive. Among the practitioners of animal magnetism whose activities were noted by the *American Phrenological Journal* was Phineas Parkhurst Quimby, who achieved remarkable results by denying the existence of physical disease entirely; his fame was to devolve upon his pupil, Mrs. Mary Baker Eddy. The *American Phrenological Journal* accepted the fact of clairvoyance, and Fowlers and Wells published many books upon spiritualism. Andrew Jackson Davis first became interested in the subject of mesmerism from hearing a lecture by James Stanley Grimes; Davis thought phrenology a great modern factor in the advance of the human race, while Emma Hardinge Britten, the spiritualist, considered it one of the "steps leading up through the once-forbidden mysteries of nature into the realm of imponderable forces, bearing the student onward to the very gates of the temple of mind, within which are now heard the low, telegraphic knocks of the spirit." [18]

In the light of modern investigations into electric brain waves, telepathy, and clairvoyance, we are inclined to be a little more charitable toward investigations of this sort. But there can be no doubt that they served further to blacken the reputation of phrenology among 19th-century scientists and intellectuals.

18. Emma Hardinge Britten, *Modern American Spiritualism* (New York, 1870), p. 22.

Chapter 12. Phrenology and Medicine

As HAS been suggested in preceding chapters, phrenology, sending its roots deep into American soil, went far beyond its European scientific foundations. Indeed, its popularity among *hoi polloi* in the United States varied directly with the length of these extrapolations. Yet the fact that public attention was focused upon the acivities of the popularizers did not mean that the original spark was thereby extinguished. Beyond and above practical phrenology there was the interest of the medical profession, which viewed the antics of the Fowlers with the same lofty disdain that Dr. Karl Menninger presumably feels for I. Ron Hubbard and his "Dianetics." Dr. Samuel Jackson, professor of physiology at the University of Pennsylvania, summed up the prevailing view:

> The doctrines of Gall embrace two general and distinct propositions which are not to be confounded. The first is, that the intellectual faculties and the cerebral organs executing them, are multiple. . . . The testimony . . . is so conclusive, that few well instructed and observing physicians, accustomed to analyze and reflect on what passes under their observation, have any difficulty in yielding accordance to this proposition.
>
> The second proposition, which is, probably, more curious than useful, is the possibility of recognizing on the exterior of the cranium, the seats of those particular organs . . . of thus acquiring, from an inspection of the cranium, a knowledge of their intellectual and moral qualification. This last proposition is far from being established.[1]

1. Samuel Jackson, *The Principles of Medicine* (Philadelphia, 1832), pp. 207–8.

To American medical men cranioscopy was a commercial fraud, and the social speculations of honorable phrenologists lay beyond their interests. Harvard's Dr. John C. Warren entertained George Combe as a scientific thinker but he did not bother to attend his lectures, since they concerned "popular and interesting topics which were, however judicious, not the information I desired." [2] The medical inquiries into phrenology went forward, as pure science always does, at an international level, and here there was no special difference between European and American attitudes.

Orson Fowler was so densely ignorant of natural science that he liked to ride the railroad because he believed it charged him with electricity, like the galvanic battery with which he was fond of dosing himself; Joseph Rodes Buchanan, wishing to be entirely original in his "research," never bothered to read the works of his predecessors. But phrenology first came to this country as a striking series of medical discoveries, based on an enormous amount of medical research and expounded in lengthy, dry, technical volumes accompanied by giant folios of illustrations, at a time when little was known and less understood about the structure and functioning of the brain. The treatises of Gall and Spurzheim were written in French and fortified by the prestige of European science, in an age when American medicine was in an extremely retarded and primitive state; Pickard and Buley dedicate their book on early American medicine to the citizen "who bravely faced the doctor." [3] Whatever the present status of Gall's exploded theories, he is still honored as a pioneer neurologist.

Therefore these works and the reports of American doctors who had studied abroad produced a great impact on the American medical profession; Isaac Ray remembered almost fifty years later that "no story-book was ever devoured with such abandon of every other thought as Gall's great work 'Sur les Fonctions.' " [4] If today the nature of thought remains an enigma and the brain itself a half-understood electrochemical mechanism, at that time American

2. Warren, *Life of John C. Warren*, 2, 13.

3. Madge E. Pickard and R. Carlyle Buley, *The Midwest Pioneer: His Ills, Cures and Doctors*, New York, 1946.

4. Capen, *Reminiscences*, p. 139.

cerebral research was simply nonexistent and the entire subject a total mystery. Into this theoretical vacuum advanced a completely logical, plausible theory, seemingly buttressed by clinical evidence which not only minutely analyzed the structure of the brain but explained its mode of operation—by analogy to the rest of the physical organs of the body in terms of specialization and localization of function. As Dr. Samuel Jackson maintained in his widely used *Principles of Medicine:*

> The phenomena of the intellect can be explained by no other systems that are satisfactory, and that are in analogy with all the other phenomena emanating from life. . . . It is utterly impossible, on any other system, and by any other principles to explain the pathological phenomena of the mind in its diseased condition. By adopting this doctrine the occurrence of these phenomena can be easily comprehended, and, by attaching the faculties of the intellect to organs, a utility is perceived, and object is determined for the complex organization of the brain and nervous system. Reject the principle, and the admirable structure of the brain is for no particular end, and its complicated arrangement without a special purpose. It is the only system placing the organization of the nervous system in harmony with the laws that prevail over the general structure of the animal economy.[5]

In other words, only the most rigorous mind would prefer agnosticism to this promise of certainty on such an important problem.

As a consequence the medical textbooks used by American doctors and students, whether of native or foreign origin, generally expounded the phrenological theories of cerebral physiology, or at least paid respectful attention to them—ignoring completely, of course, practical phrenology. For example, Robley Dunglison, Dean of the Faculty of the Jefferson Medical College of Philadelphia, in his *Human Physiology* gave a careful outline and sympathetic hearing to the system of Gall, at the same time evincing his scorn of cranioscopy. The same general position was adopted by

5. Jackson, *Principles of Medicine,* pp. 214–15.

William S. Kirkes and James Paget in *Manual of Physiology,* as
well as by "the leading text-book on physiology of its period," [6]
Human Physiology, Statistical and Dynamical, by the famous John
W. Draper. Among the manuals of British origin, Dr. John Mackintosh in *Principles of Pathology and Practice of Medicine* paid
his respects to phrenology, while the extremely detailed phrenological description of the nervous system in Dr. John Elliotson's
Physiology gave no hint that those theories might be mistaken.

Early American interest in phrenology was almost exclusively
scientific, and our first society, the Central Phrenological Society,
centered in the medical profession and included some of the most
eminent Philadelphia doctors. The *Philadelphia Medical Journal*
hoped that the European battles over the subject would not have
to be refought here: "Science, hitherto boasting of our land as an
asylum from all intolerance, finds European opposition echoed
from our shores and sounded in the valleys of the West. But each
year renders it fainter, and we shall soon hear it dying away, leaving behind it, like the summer gusts, a fairer and calmer scene." [7]
This pious hope, of course, fell short of realization, when these
reasoned defenders of Gall's validity were attacked not only by
skeptics but by the left wing of their own ranks; the fiery evangelist
Dr. Charles Caldwell bitterly criticized Dr. Samuel Jackson's calm
exposition of Gall's doctrines, already quoted, simply because he
rejected cranioscopy!

In any case, the way for Spurzheim had been prepared by the
medical interest of the 1820's, by men like Dr. John C. Warren,
who had given lectures and demonstrations of the new theories
long before Spurzheim's arrival in Boston, and who there dined
him alive and dissected him dead. Spurzheim, it should be remembered, gave a special course on the anatomy of the brain for the
benefit of the Boston Medical Society, which in its turn adopted
a special resolution in mourning and marched in a body in his
funeral procession.

Although George Combe was not a doctor, he met much the
same reception. He had learned to dissect the brain in the manner

6. Ellwood Hendrick, "John William Draper," in *DAB.*
7. *Philadelphia Medical Journal, 8* (1824), 209.

of Spurzheim—instead of cutting it straight across, the phrenologists opened it from the top and literally unfolded it, thus making its structure more clear—and this technique Combe showed to medical societies. When he demonstrated at the Albany Medical College before an audience of doctors and professors, a Dr. Hoyt came 150 miles to watch, bringing a brain with him. The aftermath of this exhibition was a hypernationalistic contretemps, an American newspaper demanding to know why American doctors had to take lessons from the British. Nevertheless, when Combe became a candidate for the chair of Logic at the University of Edinburgh, no less than sixteen prominent American doctors wrote letters on his behalf.

As noted, when Spurzheim died, the *American Journal of the Medical Sciences* cried, "The prophet is gone, but his mantle is upon us." [8] The medical journals of the United States were generally sympathetic, especially the *Boston Medical and Surgical Journal*, which enthusiastically reported Spurzheim's lectures as patronized by "the most distinguished physicians," and thereafter faithfully recounted pathological cases illustrative of phrenology. The *American Journal of Insanity* was also cordial; for instance, Dr. N. S. Davis of the New York State Asylum explained in one article why post-mortems were meaningless unless one understood the structure and function of the healthy brain, and phrenology was the only system which expounded that. If the medical journals contained many examples of phrenology, the *American Phrenological Journal* was filled with medical illustrations of cases involving brain injuries, which were sent in by doctors. The recommendation most valued by the partisans of phrenology was that in the *American Journal of Science* by Professor Benjamin Silliman, already mentioned. He maintained, among other endorsements, that "its first principles, as regards the great regions of the head, are established upon the same ground as that which sustains all the physical sciences, namely, induction, indicating the correspondence of the phenomena with the theory." [9]

In a resolution upon Spurzheim's death the Boston Medical

8. *American Journal of the Medical Sciences, 12* (1833), 473.
9. *American Journal of Science, 39* (1840), 74.

Society recommended the study of the principles of the new science to the public, since it "can no more expect to hear them from the lips of our lamented friend." [10] Suiting the action to the word, about fifty doctors became members of the new Boston Phrenological Society. Philadelphia has already been mentioned, and apparently the same situation was true of New York City, since in 1837 Dr. Amariah Brigham wrote to Nahum Capen from there: "Here I find a general and favorable impression respecting it. Nearly all the physicians are said to be phrenologists." [11] In 1841 the *American Medical Almanac* described this rising tide:

> It is impossible to estimate the numbers of believers in phrenology in this country. They may be found in every state of the union. For a few years past, the science has been rapidly advancing, as well as gaining in character and popularity. Many of the leading periodicals of the day, particularly the medical journals, take a decided stand in its favour; while others generally allude to it, whenever the occasion requires, with candour and respect. The science is now embraced by large numbers in the medical profession, especially among the younger portion. It is also favorably received by many members of the legal and clerical professions, and is beginning to be introduced and respectfully treated in our literary, scientific, and medical institutions. The day of its final triumph and general adoption cannot be far distant.[12]

There was a good deal of opposition to the new science, as we have seen, but relatively little of it was upon rational grounds or based upon legitimate evidence. Medical research in this country was virtually nonexistent, and no one was able to disprove the large amount of clinical evidence and pathological cases which the phrenologists had assembled.

The best known antagonist of the new psychology in this country was Dr. Thomas Sewall, professor of anatomy at the Columbian College of Washington, D.C., whose lectures in 1828 the Washing-

10. Capen, *Reminiscences,* p. 142.
11. *Ibid.,* p. 135.
12. Quoted in the *Phrenological Almanac* (New York, 1842), p. 38.

ton Phrenological Society attempted to challenge, as we saw in
Chapter 2. When the subject was more in the public eye (and
favor) nine years later, he published these disquisitions as a pamphlet, *An Examination of Phrenology,* and this proved so popular
that a second and enlarged edition was called for in 1839. He set
out to examine the subject scientifically and temperately, one of
the very few who did so. After an honest exposition of the principles and leading doctrines of the subject, he admitted that metaphysical arguments against it, even though "urged with great
power," had been evaded, and the lash of ridicule "has done but
little in arresting its progress." Therefore Sewall was going to try
another tack, examining its scientific accuracy. His critique con-
centrates on five points of objection: (1) the formation of the brain
does not reveal upon dissection any division into organs or com-
partments; (2) there is no necessary and unvarying relationship between the volume of the brain and the powers of the intelligence;
(3) because of the varying thickness of the cranial bones, it is impossible, even with the exact instruments used by the phrenologists, to
determine the volume of the brain; (4) because of the frontal
sinuses and the unpredictable depth of the cranial bones, the degree of the development of these various organs, even supposing
that they exist, cannot be ascertained; (5) when an area of the
brain is injured or destroyed, the faculty which is supposed to re-
side there is not correspondingly impaired.

This was hailed by the antiphrenologists as the *coup de grâce,*
but friends to science rallied in counterattack. Charles Caldwell,
as might be expected, led off with a 156-page counterblast entitled *Phrenology Vindicated and Anti-phrenology Unmasked,* in
which good sense was mixed with coarse vituperation. Dr. Sewall
entertained George Combe in Washington, and a group of Senators
and Representatives gathered to meet Combe suggested that "now
we have got phrenology and anti-phrenology fairly before us, let
us hear you fight it out." Combe gave Sewall the same explanation
he had used to convince Dr. George McClellan, founder of the
Jefferson Medical College, of the error of his ways; "he had, in
truth, created a phantom, called it phrenology, and then knocked it
down. . . . if the views to which Sewall had given the name in his

work were really phrenology, I should be altogether on his side." [13]

Sewall's first point was conceded by all students of cerebral structure, and the phrenologists never maintained the converse of counts two and three. In respect to Sewall's fourth indictment, the phrenologists admitted that in unusual cases mistakes could be made; the former's illustration of this was taken from a pathological skull which Spurzheim had brought over to demonstrate that very thing. On the other hand, Sewall's final point was crucial and later proved to be entirely true—but his evidence was weak and unconvincing. His first four points, in any case, had no relation to the phrenological theories of brain physiology and thus did not militate against medical interest in it. To the dispassionate mind, Dr. Sewall had failed to annihilate phrenology.

Nevertheless, the question cannot be ignored: what *was* wrong with phrenology? For wrong it was, in all its details, and for medical posterity its only honor, if a considerable one, is that the new doctrine drove its detractors to research and discovery in their zeal to disprove it. In 1845 Pierre Flourens by experiments with pigeon brains demonstrated that whole portions of the brain could be removed without impairment of any of the functions; in particular, that the cerebellum (where Amativeness resides) might be excised without interfering with the power of reproduction. Another French scientist, Paul Broca, in 1861 gave what is generally considered the quietus to formal phrenology by his study of aphasia, in which he showed that the faculty of speech was localized not near the eyeballs, as Gall maintained, but in another region entirely.

But the disproof of phrenology need not have waited upon experimental evidence. Localization of function exists—in a limited sense and with a few faculties—but not in the *terms* that Gall used. What apparently was not perceived at the time was that his errors were conceptual; for all his protestations of pure induction, his theories rested on a crude introspection, on the a priori assumption that the mind could be resolved into a number of independent faculties. The faculty of speech, for instance, *is* localized in a particular region of the brain. But the faculty of language, in Gall's terms, involves memory, imagination, association, abstraction,

13. Combe, *Notes*, 2, 105.

judgment, volition, and physical sounds. In other words, as William James pointed out, instead of reducing the mind to its thirty-five basic components, Gall really created thirty-five brains in miniature.[14]

The importance of phrenology in the history of neurology, we repeat, was not so much the validity of its own theories as the accumulation of experimental evidence and the direction of medical research to the problem of cerebral structure. It also had much the same effect, and an equally inadvertent one, upon another modern discipline—physical anthropology. Phrenology might have been a science with stirring moral overtones and exuberant offshoots, but it was still a science in that it appealed to nature and had a body of data. If the focus of its investigation was the brain, second to that was the skull. All partisans of the new psychology, even those learned scientists who deprecated the voluminous psychographs of the Fowlers derived from ten minute inspections, believed that *in general* the contour of the skull followed that of the brain. Generally speaking and with the exception of pathological cranial bones, unusual attributes of the human mind—insanity, the criminal type, neuroses, striking aptitudes for music or poetry (or sensuality)—were accompanied by unusual head shapes; and beyond that dictum, each of the various races of mankind had a characteristic skull formation.

The first requirement for the philosophical phrenologist, after he had mastered the principles of the science from books, was to observe nature, to put this discipline to the test; he must observe heads, notice the correlation between exceptional heads and unusual personalities. Unfortunately the desired examples were rarely encountered in everyday life, so that they had to be studied through engravings, plaster casts, and skulls. One of the necessary items of a phrenological society was a collection of several hundred samples covering all bands of the spectrum. Gall was such an assiduous collector it was said that the Viennese used to specify in their wills that their crania should be protected from his researches. His suc-

14. William James, *The Principles of Psychology* (2 vols. New York, 1902), *1*, 28–9.

cessors devised elaborate methods of taking measurements and invented the requisite instruments: callipers and cephalometers. To this measuring procedure all prominent Americans were apparently obliged to submit, judging from the encyclopedic tables published in the *American Phrenological Journal*. The Fowlers invented a quick and efficient means of making plaster casts and so were able to assemble a mighty assortment from living celebrities, famous and infamous.

The true scientist's interests were by no means exhausted by unusual examples from the white nationalities of European stock. Skulls of foreign races, especially of uncivilized tribes, were assembled, on the supposition that their phrenology would reflect their collective personalities; Gall had maintained that it is to the disposition of savages and barbarians that one must go to study the natural dispositions of the civilized nations. Even the critics of phrenology admitted that this was a fruitful line of endeavor: a writer for the *Knickerbocker* who thought the metaphysics of the new science subversive conceded that it had established "the phrenology of Nations." [15] Consequently, a knowledge of its doctrines was an obligatory item in the conceptual approach of early anthropologists, as in the analysis of the natives of Tierra del Fuego by the Beagle's surgeon, Dr. John Wilson. Another 19th-century anthropologist in a book about the Todas tribe of India announced his approach in his title, *A Phrenologist among the Todas*. [16]

Nor were the laws of mind confined to the human race. The characters of animals, too, were dictated by their brains, which were similar to man's, if on a lesser order. Gall had made some of his inferences from a study of mammals, and their skulls were supposed to be excellently illustrative of pure examples of their particular proclivities—for instance, Destructiveness in the tiger. Especially interesting were the brain chambers of the great apes, which most nearly approached those of humans. Orson Fowler advised his readers to see the orang-utang at his friend Phineas T. Barnum's establishment; it was "an intellectual treat." The *American Phrenological Journal* ran dozens of articles on the phreno-

15. *Knickerbocker, 1* (1833), 315.
16. William E. Marshall, *A Phrenologist among the Todas*, London, 1873.

logical makeup of assorted fauna, but none, unfortunately, on Melville's *jeu d'esprit,* the phrenology of the whale. At least one correspondent of that magazine used to select horses for purchase by the shape of their heads.

Because of the requirement of examples for study purposes, large collections of skulls were assembled in this country. The *American Medical Almanac,* in an 1841 article on the spread of the new science, discussed several museum collections: the Boston Phrenological Society's numbered about five hundred, its nucleus being Spurzheim's own. In 1849 Dr. John C. Warren acquired it from the society and presented it to Harvard, where it is still on exhibition at the Medical School. George Combe's collection was purchased by his last audience in New Haven; in 1841 it was "deposited in the hall of the medical department of Yale College," [17] but has now lamentably disappeared. The specimens of the Fowlers numbered about 800, including 200 of their contemporaries taken by the process previously mentioned. The Albany and Buffalo societies both had large selections, but the greatest was that of Dr. Samuel G. Morton of Philadelphia, numbering about 1,000, one-half of which were animals.

Fanny Kemble cynically reflected that George Combe would have had a great career in this country if he could have scientifically rationalized slavery, and he was often asked what light his science cast upon that burning question. His answer, frequently expounded, was a cautious one: the Negro was naturally inferior to the white in intellectual capacity because the anterior portion of his skull was somewhat narrower. But this margin did not incapacitate him for free labor and by no means justified slavery. An extensive program of Negro education was needed, and he thought the example of the freed Negroes in the North proved it.[18]

But there was another question of greater ethnological interest to Americans than even the Negro slave. Physical anthropology is peculiarly an American science, and largely because of the continuous attack upon a single problem—the eternal presence and

17. *American Phrenological Journal,* 3 (1839–40), 189.
18. Even such an ardent abolitionist as Horace Greeley believed that phrenology proved the Negro "temporarily" inferior to the white man.

challenge of the American Indian, a ferocious, "foreign," unassimilable, uncivilized, unchristianized race. Where did they come from and why do they behave as they do? What are the "Indian mounds"? Such enigmas exercised the imaginations of Americans from Samuel Sewall to Joseph Smith, and there was no issue which appeared more frequently in the journals and activities of the phrenologists. As early as 1822 Dr. Warren read a paper to a British scientific meeting interpreting phrenologically the recently excavated Indian skulls, and later he engaged Henry R. Schoolcraft to collect further examples for him, as did Toulmin Smith; W. Byrd Powell accumulated some 500 by touring the western tribes. The second issue of the Edinburgh *Phrenological Journal* had an article on the subject of the skulls, but this was corrected by Dr. Caldwell; they were the remains of a previous race driven out by the present tribes, he said. When some skulls were excavated in Massachusetts, the *East Boston Ledger* brought them to the Boston office of Fowlers and Wells for identification as authentically aboriginal. Both Spurzheim and Combe had as one of their objects in coming to this country the study of the psychology of the Indian. The verdict was that the Indian not only was mentally inferior, like the Negro, but also, because of the peculiar organization of his mental organs, was intractable and untameable.

Combe published his conclusions upon the racial characteristics of the Indian from a study of the extensive collection, before mentioned, of Dr. Samuel G. Morton, which Louis Agassiz said was alone worth a trip to America. Morton in 1839 was hard at work on his *Crania Americana,* the great pioneer work of American anthropology, which was the published description of his great collection of Indian skulls. He and his associates had already completed the detailed measurement of some ninety skulls according to phrenological principles when George Combe arrived and pointed out to them that they were working from a badly marked bust; following his advice, they threw out all the work accomplished thus far and began again, assembling by means of craniometers, callipers, dividers, and "measuring frame" sixteen different dimensions on each skull, summarizing them in statistical tables. Morton had presented the evidence that the skulls of the various tribes differed from each other, just as the collective personalities did; but he lacked a rationale to explain why this correlation should exist and to correct this omission engaged Combe to supply an appendix explaining the principles of phrenology. On the first page Morton explained that while he was convinced of the general theory of phrenology, he was still a "learner" and so had commissioned Combe, its most famous exponent, to supply that section. Not yet converted to craniology, Morton admitted, however, "a singular harmony" between the typical cranium of the Indian and his character as explained by this new psychology. He also acknowledged his debt to the writings of Drs. Caldwell and Warren and other phrenologists.

Crania Americana was an epoch-making book; Benjamin Silliman wrote in his own copy "a *great* work" and gave it a thirty-four-page review in the *American Journal of Science*. The "unphilosophical prejudice" of attacking or defending any work of physiology according to one's own views on phrenology had been too long indulged, he said; here was this system put to practical use, with "phrenological facts and inferences . . . presented passim." [19] The net result was the "most extensive and valuable contribution to the natural history of man, which has yet appeared on the American continent," and in this virgin field which Morton had explored "the phrenologist alone can claim precedence of him." [20]

But the attitudes of the intellectuals toward phrenology shifted rapidly in this decade, because of the popularization and charlatanism of the practical phrenologists, and as the intellectual weather shifted, a permanent cloud of disrepute passed across the fair face of Combe's science. If Benjamin Silliman in 1840 could be proud of its seminal influence upon Morton's work, only fourteen years later one of Morton's associates felt compelled to apologize and excuse it:

A new impetus had been given, however, to the speciality of Craniology by the promulgation of the views of Gall and Spurzheim, then creating their greatest excitement. These distin-

19. *American Journal of Science, 38* (1839–40), 375.
20. *Ibid.,* p. 353.

guished persons completed the publication of their great work
in Paris in 1819, both before and after which time Spurzheim
lectured in Great Britain, making many proselytes. The phrenologists must have been in the very fervor of their first love
during Morton's residence there, and they included in their
number some men of genuine ability and eloquence. Collections of prepared crania, of casts and masks, became common;
but they were brought together in the hope of illustrating
character, not race, and were prized as if a fanciful hypothesis
could make their protuberances correspond with the distribution of intellectual faculties in a most crude and barren psychology. Morton's collection was ethnographic in its aim from
the outset; nor can I find that he ever committed himself fully
to the miscalled Phrenology—a system based on principles in-
disputably true, but which it holds in common with the world
of science at large, while all that is peculiar to itself is already
fading into oblivion. Attractive by its easy comprehensibility
and facility of application, it acquired a sudden and widespread
popularity, and so passed out of the hands of the men of science,
step by step, till it has now become the property of ignorant
charlatans, describing characters for twenty-five cents a head.
The very name is so degraded by these associations, that we are
apt to forget that . . . it had its effect . . . upon the mind of
Morton.[21]

21. Henry S. Patterson, "Memoir of the Life and Scientific Labors of
Samuel George Morton," in J. C. Nott and George R. Gliddon, *Types of
Mankind* (Philadelphia, 1855), pp. xxii–xxiii.

Chapter 13. Phrenology and Religion

But I deny that there exists between phrenology and the supernatural or marvelous portion of Revealed Religion, the shadow of relation, direct or indirect, by inference or otherwise.

Dr. Charles Caldwell, 1839

Dr. Brigham seems to be an infidel as well as a phrenologist. Query: Did his phrenological principles *make* him a skeptic?—NO.

Yale undergraduate (?), ca. 1840 [1]

THERE is little evidence that the medical indictments of phrenology had any considerable impact upon the popular mind. In a prescientific age the question of medical validity was subordinate to social and ethical utility; most interested Americans, so it appears, soon made up their minds about this plausible and attractive doctrine and then utilized the anatomical evidence brought forward to rationalize their verdicts, favorable or unfavorable. When Flourens made what seems, at least to 20th-century eyes, a most devastating attack, the *Southern Literary Messenger* merely dismissed him as a "canting reviler of Gall." [2] The rhetoric was inflated but, oddly enough, the judgment essentially fair. Flourens was no closeted researcher, since he announced in his introduction, "I am writing in opposition to a bad philosophy, while I am endeavoring to recall a sound one," [3] by which he meant liberty and the philosophy of Descartes, to whom he dedicated his books. Dr. Charles D. Meigs, Professor of Obstetrics at the Jefferson Medical

1. Handwritten comment on the title page of the Yale Library copy of David M. Reese, *Phrenology Known by Its Fruits,* New York, 1836.
2. *Southern Literary Messenger, 12* (1846), 272.
3. Pierre Flourens, *Phrenology Examined* (Philadelphia, 1846), pp. viii–ix.

College, wrote in his translator's preface that he was bringing this work to the American public not as a contribution to medicine but because he feared "the influence of false metaphysics" upon "the juror, the judge, and the legislator." [4]

The phrenologists had deserted the laboratory for the arena of mundane affairs; since their orientation was deliberately social, they were judged by the nonrational standards of society at large. The most common and successful attacks were inflamed and emotional appeals to evangelical Protestantism—the real message of this new science, according to its critics, was atheism, materialism, and determinism; the real casualties were moral responsibility and free will. The partisans of the new psychology, on the other hand, gave as good as they took, in the same tone and in the same vein. Their rejoinders, equally inflammatory and irrational, cast more heat than light. It was in vain that Benjamin Silliman asked for "a suspension of hostilities preliminary to an amicable and fair discussion of the points at issue," [5] or that the *New World* called the charge of infidelity "foolish and bigoted." [6] It was a religiously minded age (in the broadest sense), the point of departure was theological, and for that reason much of the discussion today seems irrelevant; we tend to sympathize with Emerson's complaint about a phrenological lecture he heard: "these eternal preliminaries . . . this removing of objections which did not exist. . . ." [7]

The religious argument against phrenology reiterated the following counts: if phrenological concepts were true, character consisted of nothing more than the relative development of a number of organs, brought into play by external influences. Thus there was no human freedom, since thought, volition, and emotion were merely actions of the brain. Such a mind could not conceive of a First Cause or anything immaterial; experience and physical laws could be the only universals worthy of intellectual respect. Since man was a sort of intellectual machine, and thought a function of

4. *Ibid.*, p. xiv.

5. Benjamin Silliman, *Phrenology* (New Haven, 1840), p. 23 (reprint of Silliman's article in the *American Journal of Science;* see above, p. 147, n. 19).

6. *New World, 3* (1841), 123.

7. Rusk, *Letters of Ralph Waldo Emerson, 1,* 407.

the mechanism, he was not responsible for his action to God; in fact, the study of comparative anatomy having revealed his close relationship to the animals, he could hardly be called of divine origin. If these animadversions upon phrenology made mankind less divine, in the same breath the pulpit could argue that the omission of original sin and total corruption made the human species godlike, with no need for spiritual guidance.

These charges were rung in varying keys in sermons and religious magazines all through the Middle Period. Much of the invective, of course, may be charged simply to the clergy's dislike of innovation and suspicion of science in all its various forms. This aspect the phrenologists hailed as one more episode in that never-ending conflict between science and religion and sought to link arms with their equally embattled brethren in geology and astronomy. But it is not just to attribute all the opposition to the ministry, which was after all spokesman for the profound interest of a church-going age; Benjamin Silliman, for example, notwithstanding his serene mediation and scholarly judiciousness, anxiously directed a private inquiry to Combe of whether he believed in Christianity. Combe reported that the "most numerous conversations" [8] after his lectures were about the logical consequences of his teachings upon religion and morality.

The phrenologists met these headlong attacks in varying ways. Sometimes they simply denied the opposition of their science to conventional religion as "a most unreasonable and unfounded charge," in the words of Thomas W. Olcott in his presidential address to the Albany Phrenological Society.[9] Edward Hitchcock, friend of Benjamin Silliman and Amos Eaton, pointed out in his inaugural address on becoming president of Amherst that phrenology did not really impinge upon the question of materialism, since "it is as easy to see how an immaterial soul should act through a hundred organs as through one." [10]

8. Combe, *Notes, 1,* 210.

9. Thomas W. Olcott, *Address to the Albany Phrenological Society* (Albany, 1840), p. 6.

10. Edward Hitchcock, *Religious Truth, Illustrated from Science, in Addresses and Sermons on Special Occasions* (Boston, 1857), p. 40.

More often the defense was indirect, claiming that instead of conflicting or competing, in reality Christianity and phrenology complemented and reinforced each other. Early statements of this genre appeared in the works of John Epps, a member of the Edinburgh Phrenological Society: *Internal Evidences of Christianity, Deduced from Phrenology* and *Horae Phrenologicae;* both were reprinted in Boston in the 1830's. An American follower of Epps was William Ingalls, professor of medicine at Brown College, who wrote *Phrenology Not Opposed to the Principles of Religion: nor the Precepts of Christianity;* his practical experience with the science had been derived from visits to the institutions of Samuel Gridley Howe and Samuel B. Woodward. The two American editions of Epps were edited by the Reverend Joseph A. Warne and the Reverend John Pierpont, respectively. The former added a chapter to one edition of *The Constitution of Man,* "On the Harmony between the Scriptures and Phrenology"; because this particular edition was destined for the libraries of the New York public schools, it was felt that an additional safeguard was necessary. The Reverend Pierpont, fiery reformer, poet, and grandfather to J. P. Morgan, battled with his congregation over the attention he paid to "two imported mountebanks" (Spurzheim and Combe), to whom he said he was "more indebted for instruction in the philosophy of mind . . . than to all other men, living or dead." [11] His contribution to the great debate was *Phrenology and the Scriptures,* which indicated the analogies and the impossibility of contradiction between the two teachings.

The early society periodicals were extremely cautious and at pains to conciliate orthodoxy. The *Annals of Phrenology* maintained not only that its discipline did not teach materialism, but that its coincidence with Christianity was exact, and furthermore, God and Jesus were phrenologically perfect! The same conformity was evinced by the original *American Phrenological Journal,* under the editorial direction of Nathan Allen, who announced in his manifesto that the policy of the new publication would be, in contrast to certain other partisans of the science, "decidedly evangeli-

11. Combe, *Notes, 3,* 171.

cal." [12] Nelson Sizer could not have been one of the unevangelical partisans Allen referred to: the Reverend Noah Porter, father of Yale's future president, took him into his home for an interview and thought his mode of presentation "would be a decided assistance to him in stemming the influence of infidelity." [13]

Orson Fowler focused his original mind and prose style on the problem, with the customary original results. In 1843 he published *The Christian Phrenologist*, a lecture delivered before the Lyceum at Cazenovia, N.Y., and followed this the next year with a full-scale work entitled *Religion, Natural and Revealed*, the preface of which typically states: "how all-absorbing the interest, how overwhelming the importance, how momentous the results of a comparison of the religion of phrenology with the religion of the Bible! My pen falters! *Must* I proceed?" [14] But proceed he did, and God and religion, if not the Old Testament, came out of it pretty well; not only did he by teleological evidence confirm morality and immortality, but by a curious circular argument established the existence of God—if there were no God, what was the organ of Veneration for?

This did not mean that any substantial proportion of the clergy looked with favor on the proselytizing activities of the new science, or, for that matter, that they had any reason to do so. Nor were the actions of the phrenologists devoted solely to the proofs of the identity of their teachings with those of orthodox Protestantism and its ministers. Between the two camps there was mutual antipathy, varying with individuals, and in reality it was difficult to reconcile phrenology with conventional evangelicanism. The *American Phrenological Journal* admitted that "the one great obstacle" has been the opposition of the clergy *"as a class"* [15] and in every issue carried highly partisan accounts of the struggle. Sometimes the indictment was upon the science as a whole, at other times

12. *American Phrenological Journal, 1* (1838–39), 7.

13. Sizer, *Forty Years in Phrenology*, p. 211.

14. Orson S. Fowler, *Religion, Natural and Revealed* (New York, 1843), p. viii.

15. *American Phrenological Journal, 23* (1856), 2.

it was directed to single individuals, viz. Walter Edgerton's *A Brief Review of Certain Phrenological Works of O. S. Fowler.*

The opposition of the clergy was neither inconsistent nor un-provoked, for the hostility of most partisans of the new science was patent. Of Dr. Epps' gentle attempt at mediation Orson Fowler wrote "I despise this truckling to existing prejudices. . . . Christianity I also admire, (not *modern* Christianity, or rather the modern *perversions* of Christianity, but the Christianity of the *Bible*,) and I think I discover a perfect *similarity* between the two; but phrenology shows up some of the notions engrafted upon Christianity by modern sects in a clear and exposing light. It is also destined to do much to *reform* Christianity, or rather modern *bigotry.*" [16] He attacked ceremonies, creeds, sects, the efficacy of prayer, and most of all, bigoted, obscurantist, conservative (and, of course, antiphrenologist) ministers. Like Puritans the proponents of this system of psychology thought it would literally reform and purify Christianity by excision of some modern additions and by reversion to the pristine purity of early Christianity.

Although Orson Fowler resided well out toward the thickly populated lunatic fringe of phrenology, this tendency was true of all the leaders. George Combe was eagerly cross-examined by his auditors about what happened to the doctrine of total corruption if men were naturally good, and what happened to Christian retribution if "habitual criminals" were to be regarded only as unfortunates and "moral patients"; his answers were that the first question was only for those who believed in total corruption and as to the second, men must bring their interpretations of Scripture "into harmony with natural truth." [17] In this same connection he showed interest and agreement with Yale Professor Nathaniel W. Taylor's abandonment of total corruption.

This tolerant and rationalistic approach to religion sometimes came close to complete indifference. Piety itself was the result of the action of a single organ, that of Veneration; therefore "devout" and "virtuous" were not necessarily synonymous, since a person might be "greatly interested in acts of devotion but very

16. *Ibid., 4* (1842), 222.
17. Combe, *Notes, 1,* 208.

little addicted to honesty and goodness." [18] E. P. Hurlbut, an American judge writing upon the right of religious freedom according to phrenological theory, thought that a person entirely destitute of religious feeling was "a very eccentric person. Perhaps that is the worst that ought to be said about him." [19] Dr. Amariah Brigham, in his *Influence of Religion on Health and Welfare,* maintained that the Indians could not be converted because of the quality of their brains and quoted Dr. Charles Caldwell to prove that religious divisions, sectarian strife, and revivals were the cause of much insanity. Dr. David M. Reese wrote a 195-page book entitled *Phrenology Known by Its Fruits,* reviewing Brigham's work, which he said should have been entitled "Observations on the Influence of Religion in Producing Wars, Bloodshed, Sickness, Insanity, and Death." [20]

Gall and Spurzheim, it should be remembered, were avowed deists, and George Combe came to phrenology only after a profound struggle with the Calvinism of his youth. Thereafter he gave up all belief in a personal God and said that in his book about America he intended to "speak pretty freely of Calvinism and its effects on the mind." [21] Fanny Kemble reported both the Combes as "much more aggressive . . . with regard to 'Church abuses,' 'theological bigotry,' and even Christianity itself." [22] He looked closely to discover the extent of infidelity in this country, but with inconclusive results.

Although Combe's emphasis on moral government put him outside the free-thought ranks, the partisans of atheism still regarded his arguments against a special Providence and against the efficacy of prayer as powerful weapons. Any attempt to explain human behavior in physiological terms was of deep interest to organized infidelity, and free-thought periodicals frequently contained articles on phrenology and advertisements of books on the subject. Abner Kneeland's Boston *Investigator* kept phrenological

18. *Ibid.,* 2, 213.
19. *Phrenological Journal,* 19 (1846), 29.
20. Reese, *Phrenology Known by Its Fruits,* p. 46.
21. Gibbon, *Combe,* 2, 78.
22. Kemble, *Recollections,* p. 542.

books for sale "as [phrenology] is becoming more and more interesting to the public," [23] while William Vale, editor of the *New
York Beacon,* was a believer and frequently published articles on it.
When Dr. Charles Knowlton was released after a jail sentence for
his notorious pioneering activities on behalf of birth control, he
cited as evidence for his materialistic ideas the teachings of Gall
and Spurzheim. The Fanny Wright–Robert Dale Owen free-
thought group used to hold running debates on the subject. The
works of George Combe, naturally enough, were placed on the
Catholic Index. It was significant that the anonymous author of
Vestiges of the Natural History of Creation (1845), that remarkable
anticipation of Darwinism, accepted phrenology as the philosophy
of man, "the only one founded upon nature"; [24] at first the authorship was attributed to George Combe, for whom it possessed "all
the sublimity of a grand poem, and the sober earnestness and per-
spicuity of a rigidly philosophical induction." [25]

In Great Britain the tension between the two wings of phrenology—one maintaining a belief in theism and some form of
spiritual essence, the other supporting complete materialism—
finally built up to a complete break and the establishment of a
new magazine to serve the strict rationalists. Its manifesto accused
the opposing party of pursuing "an equivocal and cowardlike policy . . . the anomalous spectacle of inductive philosophers wear-
ing the dress of mystagogues," because they had never "dared to
declare what your science teaches, *that the actions of the human
race necessarily result from their organic constitution.*" As for
the schismatics, they would indulge in no "metaphysical speculation," would postulate no essence, for which "we have no evidence," and would face the fact that "organized matter is all that
is requisite to produce the manifestations of human and brute
cerebration," and that "man differs from other beings only in
possessing a superior organization." [26] The young phrenologist

23. Boston *Investigator,* March 27, 1835, p. 2.
24. *Vestiges of the Natural History of Creation* (New York, 1845), p. 239.
25. Gibbon, *Combe,* 2, 146.
26. *Zoist, 1* (1843), 9, 12, 14.

Herbert Spencer, needless to say, affiliated with the radicals and wrote articles for their magazine.

In this country, however, the phrenologists never broke over the question of religion. Instead of being specifically antireligious, their cult was rather a substitute for orthodoxy, a kind of church of its own, like Unitarianism or Universalism, both of which it much resembled. Far from driving its sectaries to free thought, it rather saved them from it. To quote two of Orson Fowler's admirers: "Phrenology saved me from the rock of infidelity on which I had struck. . . . When I saw, that the mind was *constitutionally* adapted to the great and leading principles of Christianity, I was enabled to comprehend the fallacy of the base and servile doctrines of the infidel." [27] "In my distress, I turned my attention to phrenology . . . for salvation from universal scepticism's painful confusion's derangement—which last I very much feared. And blessed be God. . . . all my doubts and perplexities fled like morning vapors chased away by the rising sun." [28]

Instead of attacking religion and carrying materialism to its logical conclusion, American phrenology became a sort of religion itself, a kind of optimistic and sentimental deism. It appropriated the logic and techniques of evangelical Protestantism—its lecturers received a "call" to the "faith," designated themselves "missionaries," conducted "revivals," distributed "tracts," and made "converts." Here is the description by a "convert" of the new Godhead which his science has revealed to him; the vocabulary may be a little odd, but the lineaments of his God are the familiar ones of mid 19th-century America:

> Whereas he formerly regarded his Maker as a mere tyrant, whom it was almost impossible to please—one who was so very jealous of our affections, and one who so delighted in our destruction, as to seek every opportunity to discover a defect in our conduct, that he might have some excuse to consign us to everlasting punishment. But once the glorious light of phre-

27. Fowler, *Religion, Natural and Revealed*, p. 119.
28. *Ibid.*, pp. 124–5.

nology has dawned upon his dark and benighted mind, and dispelled the dismal clouds that had hung over it, it beholds his Maker in quite a different light. He now looks upon him as a kind, benevolent, and all-wise Father, one who delights in the happiness of his children—one who is moved, by disinterested love, to sympathize with us in all our sufferings, and who is ever ready to guide us by his unerring wisdom, in the ways of holiness and heaven.[29]

29. *American Phrenological Journal,* 24 (1856), 131.

PART THREE. CONCLUSION

Chapter 14. Phrenology and the American Spirit

Human History is in essence a history of ideas . . . of states of mind and of acts arising out of them.

H. G. Wells

Ideology may tend to hurry men forward, if it happens to accord with the wind and tide of circumstance; otherwise, if effective at all, it may momentarily weaken the play of natural forces. But the idea that hurries men forward did not set them upon that route; they invented the idea or adopted it because it expressed their existing purpose or activity.

Edward McC. Sait

Still, must not every such psycho-sociological movement, dangerous or fantastic as it may be, meet some public need in order to "catch on"? Further, what is there about our age that causes such a widespread confusion of science, faith, and fiction—a confusion shown in the public reaction to the "flying saucers" phenomenon and the popularity of "Worlds in Collision" as well as dianetics?

Rollo May, 1951

IN 1851 a journalist named Emerson Davis wrote a book called *The Half Century*, reviewing the progress of the past fifty fruitful years, in the same manner as would Alfred Russell Wallace at the end of the century. After examining the remarkable progress in the various fields of science and technology, he summarized the methods and conclusions of phrenology and cast a skeptical eye upon its claims: "What practical principle has it discovered? It has been investigated and examined for fifty years, and what important change has it wrought? What good has it done? In what walk of usefulness can its footsteps be traced?" [1]

A century later those questions are even more difficult to an-

1. Emerson Davis, *The Half Century* (Boston, 1851), p. 265.

swer. Concrete results there were: an interest in skulls and brain structure, an appreciation of the significance of insane asylums and penitentiaries, a tendency toward octagonal architecture and against whipping pupils. But these were inevitable, probably, and would have come without the noisy advocacy of the phrenologists. The significance of phrenology lies rather in its philosophy, for the whole was something more than the sum of its parts. Like Darwinism, phrenology left the laboratory and thereafter its "proof" lay in debating forums and public acceptance, not in scientific experiments. Thomas Mann once said that Freud was more important as a philosopher than as a scientist, and the same could be said of Gall, although he, like Darwin, would have been astounded at some of the deductions popularizers drew from his theories.

That it was a social *philosophy* and was regarded as such by contemporaries all observers agree. James Wadsworth, of the famous New York family, told Combe that he had given a new religion to the world; "the views of the Divine government there unfolded will in time subvert all other religions and become a religion themselves. . . . I call it Combeism." [2] Its enthusiasts, as well as its critics, insisted on discussing the discipline not as a science or a body of data but as a philosophy, and especially as a philosophy which did not require the effort or capacity for rigorous abstract thinking. John Chambers, of *Chambers' Journal,* pointed out that "phrenology is eminently the system of mental philosophy for the unlearned man, because it is much less abstract than any other. . . . ordinary people feel, for the first time . . . they have ground whereon to rest the soles of their feet." [3] The epigraph of Mrs. L. Miles' *Phrenology, and the Moral Influence of Phrenology,* which Edgar Allan Poe thought such a great contribution to knowledge, was "it is not necessary to be either a metaphysician or an

2. Gibbon, *Combe, 2,* 74.

3. *American Phrenological Journal, 14* (1857), title page. See also the *American Monthly Review, 3* (1833), 422: "Multitudes that would never dream of embracing any system which they supposed to require profound, searching, and unwearied thought . . . will eagerly snatch at phrenology as opening a royal road, easy and short, into the very depths of metaphysics and morals."

anatomist in order to understand phrenology." [4] It is significant that the prominent men who embraced it, famous though they might have been, were basically incapable of deep philosophical thought and emotionally seized upon these new doctrines as a sort of short cut to metaphysics. Horace Mann confessed himself "a hundred times more indebted to phrenological than to all the metaphysical works I ever read." [5] Henry Ward Beecher proclaimed that it underlaid his whole ministry and recommended as the best preparation for a Christian "a practical knowledge of the human mind as is given by phrenology." [6] Charles Caldwell revealed more than he intended, when he proudly declared "of all the systems I have examined, that of Gall and Spurzheim is the only one I can either believe or understand. As soon would I bind myself to discover the philosopher's stone, or to concoct the elixer of life out of simples, as to find substantial meaning in many of the tenets of fashionable metaphysics." [7] Even so intelligent a critic as James Freeman Clarke, Boston's famous Unitarian minister and Transcendentalist, maintained even in his old age that Spurzheim's visit had been beneficial, since "metaphysics, a doubtful, uncertain study heretofore, with small practical results, at once became interesting and adapted to daily use." [8] Samuel Gridley Howe paid the same dubious compliment: "The mind is taxed and strained to the utmost to follow the metaphysical authors, and mystical psychologists through their abstruse speculations; and many an unsatisfactory headache have I had as the only reward of such effort; but phrenology—it is clear, simple, natural: he who runs may read; and every reader may comprehend." [9]

But cynics pointed with scorn to this "virtue" of which phrenology's partisans were so proud; for instance, Dr. John Augustine

4. Mrs. L. Miles, *Phrenology and the Moral Influence of Phrenology*, title page.

5. *American Phrenological Journal*, 25 (1857), title page.

6. Capen, *Reminiscences*, p. 157.

7. *Phrenological Journal*, 9 (1834–36), 480–1.

8. James Freeman Clarke, *Autobiography, Diary and Correspondence*, ed. Edward Everett Hale (Boston, 1891), p. 48.

9. Howe, *Address*, p. 18.

Smith, Professor at New York's College of Physicians and Surgeons: "no nice distinctions to puzzle—no abstractions to bewilder —no insuperable barriers to circumscribe his acquaintance, and mortify his vanity. . . . Let him observe the head, consult the chart—summon the genius of phrenology—that is, invoke his imagination, and there bursts upon the mind—all that phrenology can teach him." [10] Frederick H. Hedge, the leader of the Transcendentalists, made the same point in even more scorching language:

> Meanwhile its prevalence among the unlearned is easily accounted for. A philosophy of some sort,—a philosophy of human nature, which, whether true or false, may be paraded and talked about, is a luxury to which in these days, almost everyone aspires. But unluckily, a system of philosophy was till lately a difficult acquisition. The aspirant was forced, either to turn his attention within himself—a very uninteresting employment; or else to read books which required some degree of mental application—an unpleasant alternative. But now there springs up a system which requires no such hard conditions; —a philosophy which appeals simply and solely to the senses, and therefore suited to the humblest capacity and coarsest taste; a philosophy which lays out human nature in the form of a map, so that every man, woman, or child, who will take the trouble to spend a few hours over that map, and learn the names of its different provinces, with their respective locations, may rise up a philosopher, completely versed with the noble science of man. [11]

Any assessment of the role of this popular philosophy in America inevitably involves a comparison with its cultural context. And the surprising fact emerges that, disregarding their circuitous reasoning and bizarre terminology, the phrenologists arrived at just about the same conclusions as other Americans. If Orestes Brown-

10. John Augustine Smith, *Predilections on Some of the More Important Subjects Connected with Moral and Physical Science* (New York, 1853), p. 141.
11. *Christian Examiner, 17* (1834), 268.

son accepted phrenology as a science but not a philosophy, most
others felt precisely the opposite, including some of its bitterest
critics. Combe says he was advised that his lectures on education
were "so sound and luminous that I should have done much more
good if I had omitted phrenology, and delivered them simply as
founded on common sense." [12] Oliver Wendell Holmes, despite
his sarcastic attacks on this "pseudo-science," still remembered
twenty-five years later his enjoyment of hearing "the dry-fibred but
human-hearted George Combe teach good sense under the disguise
of his equivocal system." [13] In 1831 William Ellery Channing reported as the consensus on *The Constitution of Man:* "the common remark, however, is that the book is excellent, in spite of its
phrenology." [14] When Richard Cobden first read the same work, it
seemed to him "like a transcript of his own familiar thoughts." The
American Annals of Education noted that readers "will learn too
the interesting fact, that the new science of which Dr. Spurzheim
was one of the parents, confirms the opinions which were formed,
before its origin, from general views of human nature, in regard
to the best manner of preparing man for his present duties, and his
future destiny." [15] As we have seen, the scientific basis of phrenology was neglected and only half-understood; it was the vitality
of its philosophical principles rather than the strength of its physiological scaffolding that attracted converts and protracted its life.

The teachings of these new doctrines did not deeply affect the
morality of everyday life, it should be noted. Like Unitarianism,
Universalism, and Transcendentalism, phrenology taught that so-
briety and virtue, chastity and self-improvement were the keys to
the good life. The musty earnestness of its books preached self-
culture and self-improvement to such a degree that they read like
parodies of Dale Carnegie. According to James Simpson, George
Combe had actually demonstrated, in capital letters, "THAT THE
WORLD IS ACTUALLY ARRANGED ON THE PRINCIPLE OF FAVOURING

12. Combe, *Notes, 3,* 175–6.
13. Holmes, *Writings, 9,* 245.
14. Gibbon, *Combe, 1,* 221.
15. *American Annals of Education, 3* (1833), 128.

VIRTUE AND PUNISHING VICE." [16] Any science which set out to demonstrate so safe a thesis was in tune with the national music of the United States.

The great vogue of phrenology was during the Middle Period, which was characterized by social ferment, the rise of the common man, and the decline of Calvinism. In this era three leitmotivs were dominant in American thought—the moral law, the free individual, the mission of America [17]—and these the phrenologist extolled so explicitly and strenuously as almost to parody them.

Phrenology, in one sense, was no more than a plea for man to live in accordance with the moral law; as Combe wrote to Channing, the proper function of religion was to direct the mind "to the legitimate use of man's functions as being the true will of God, to every abuse of these as being transgressions of that will." [18] And that was why sectarian religion, existing systems of education and penology, and the use of liquor and confining dress were wrong and must be reformed: they were violations of this moral order and natural constitution which God had established and which man had only to follow in order to achieve happiness and salvation.

It was a philosophy of extreme individualism, for the free individual. The new science allied itself with virtually every one of the various reform movements of the 1830's and 1840's, but there was one type of which it specifically disapproved—the various collectivist experiments, such as Brook Farm and the Fourierist Phalanxes. Combe wrote articles attacking socialism, for the phrenologists believed that salvation lay not in it but in more education for the masses. This extreme individualism emphasized each man's individual endowment and set of capacities, by means of which he could lift himself with the aid of phrenological science. On the title page of Orson Fowler's books was inscribed his motto: "Self-made or never made." Under the pseudonym of "A Phrenologist," E. P.

16. James Simpson, *Necessity of Popular Education as a National Object; with Hints on the Treatment of Criminals, and Observations on Homicidal Insanity* (Edinburgh, 1834), p. 44.

17. Ralph H. Gabriel, *The Course of American Democratic Thought* (New York, 1940), pp. 14–25.

18. Gibbon, *Combe, 1,* 220.

Hurlbut, judge of the Supreme Court of New York and vice-president of the New York Phrenological Society, wrote an article for the *Democratic Review* on phrenological principles, entitled "On Rights and Government"; in it he attacked Bentham and stood fast on the old doctrine of Natural Rights: "The Sovereign of the universe has legislated for man; has stamped His laws upon the moral constitution; and, thus provided, man enters the social state, to pursue happiness in obedience to the laws of his organization, needing nothing from human legislation but the protection of his natural Rights." [19]

It was only in America where men were allowed to be free, to govern themselves, to make that inevitable progress toward the moral order. It was the example and the mission of America that made Europe, oppressed by decadent monarchy and deadly conservatism, revolt in 1848: "our example, our prosperity have stirred up . . . an uncontrollable desire to progress in like manner. . . . the more perfectly we fulfill our destiny, the sooner will every nation, and kindred, and tongue, and sect, and individual, upon the whole earth, be brought out of the present kingdom of sin and suffering into that of virtue and happiness. Our nation is the world's leaven, and the better we make it the sooner will the human mass become leavened." [20] Phrenology was a humane and optimistic faith, believing in the perfectibility of America as well as man, and even Combe had this interesting reservation to make on Tocqueville's *Democracy in America:*

> The only point in which I perceive a deficiency is a want of a philosophy of mind that might have enabled him to penetrate more clearly into the future. In the United States a vast moral experiment is in progress. He perceives its magnitude and importance, and the embarrassments with which it is beset; but he does not equally well appreciate the relation in which the phenomena stand to the human faculties, or divine their ulti-

19. *United States Magazine and Democratic Review, 9* (1841), 583. Hurlbut's ideas are expanded in his *Essays on Human Rights and Their Political Guaranties,* New York, 1845.

20. *American Phrenological Journal, 11* (1849), 12, 31.

mate effect on American civilization. The reader rises from
the perusal of his work embarrassed by fears and doubts. It appears to me that phrenology enables us to dispel much darkness
from the horizon, and to view the future progress of the United
States in a more favourable light than that in which it is regarded in his pages.[21]

Thus American minds were already conditioned to the acceptance of this new science. And phrenology was itself reshaped, far
from its British counterpart, and farther still from the aristocratic
philosophy of Gall, to its peculiar utilitarian and optimistic configuration. It is a permissible generalization that it provided a "scientific" rationalization, of which Americans were already convinced,
of the infinite improvability and perfectibility of man. Or it might
be said of phrenology, as Carl Becker said of Locke, that it allowed
its advocates to believe what they wanted to believe.

Yet it would be superficial to assign phrenology the purely negative role of a foreign echo and European affirmation of a native
American ideology. Men do not crusade for platitudes, nor do they
war on truisms. That some of the ideas of this new science were
already implicit in the American experiment does not mean that
they all were; with all the smoke of controversy there must have
been some genuine conflagration. Phrenology did not merely docu-
ment some native American ideals—it accentuated and exaggerated
them, while some of its really radical concepts gained acceptance
from association with it. In Mannheim's terminology, phrenology
was "Utopia" as well as "Ideology."

In some ways it was a really novel and striking social philosophy. It underscored the role of heredity, to the violent disapproval
of Robert Dale Owen, and the varying endowments of men and
their differentiation; thus it emphasized individualism and the
doctrine of liberty synonymous with it. Yet it escaped the anti-
democratic implications of this emphasis by neatly balancing
against it the function of environment, the doctrine of the growth
of the faculties through exercise, which came close to anticipating
John B. Watson's behaviorism. Thus, if men were not equal, by

21. Combe, *Notes*, *3*, 15–16.

scientific training they could all be brought to equal grades of perfection; and by this bridge the phrenologist could believe in both liberty and substantial equality, in both laissez-faire and democracy. As James Freeman Clarke recollected in his old age,

> One of the real benefits of this study was that it inspired courage and hope in those who were depressed by the consciousness of some inability. . . . Phrenology also showed us how, as Goethe says, our virtues and vices grow out of the same roots; how every tendency has its danger, and every dangerous power may be so restrained and guided as to be a source of good. It explained that the organic tendencies in themselves have no moral quality, but become virtues and vices as they are guided or neglected by the higher spiritual powers. These distinctions were of great value and aided us, quite apart from any judgement on the truth or error of the system.[22]

By inspiring hope in those conscious of their own deficiencies, it thus was a vehicle of optimism. This humane and engaging faith, of course, afforded to the rising sects of Unitarianism, Universalism, and Methodism a weapon with which to attack the total corruption and original sin of a decaying Calvinism. Finally, it was a "safe" radicalism—permissible within a constitutional frame of government because it preached reform rather than revolution—to advocate that each man should reform and develop himself rather than merge with his class and throw up the barricades.

In this era there was a great faith in education; as Edward Everett Hale wrote of his youth, "there was the real impression that the Kingdom of Heaven was to be brought in by teaching people what were the relations of acids to alkalies, and what was the derivation of the word 'cordwainer.' If we only knew enough, it was thought we should be wise enough to keep out of the fire and should not be burned." [23] In such a setting the novelty and the direct experimental approach to psychological problems had a tremendous impact, much like that of Freud's almost a century

22. Clarke, *Autobiography*, p. 49.
23. Edward Everett Hale, *A New England Boyhood* (New York, 1893), p. 26.

later. This statement of Walter Lippmann's strikes a familiar note: "When I compare his [Freud's] work with the psychology I studied in college or with most of the work that is used to controvert him, I cannot help feeling that for his illumination, for his steadiness and brilliance of mind, he may rank among the greatest who have contributed to thought." [24] John Morley explained George Combe's influence on Richard Cobden in somewhat the same fashion:

> That memorable book [*The Constitution of Man*] whose principles have now, in some shape or other, become the accepted commonplaces of all rational persons, was a startling revelation when it was first published in 1828. . . . We cannot wonder that zealous men were found to bequeath fortunes for the dissemination of that wholesome gospel; that it was circulated by scores of thousands of copies, and that it was seen on shelves where there was nothing else save the Bible and Pilgrim's Progress.[25]

In the second half of the century the Transcendentalists wrote their autobiographies and, strangely enough, paid their respects to what was by that time known as an exploded pseudoscience. James Freeman Clarke's has already been quoted; Emerson remembered "a certain sharpness of criticism, an eagerness for reform, which showed itself in every quarter. . . . Gall and Spurzheim's phrenology laid a rough hand on the mysteries of animal and spiritual nature, dragging down every sacred secret to a street show. The attempt . . . had a certain truth in it; it felt connection where the professors denied it, and was leading to a truth which had not yet been announced." [26] Theodore Parker's recollections are in the same vein: "Besides, the phrenologists, so ably represented by Spurzheim and Combe, were weakening the power of the old supernaturalism, leading men to study the constitution of man more

24. *New Republic,* 2 (1915), Supplement, pp. 9–10.
25. John Morley, *The Life of Richard Cobden* (Boston, 1881), p. 63.
26. Ralph Waldo Emerson, *Complete Works* (12 vols. Boston, Riverside edition, 1897–1900), *10,* 318.

wisely than before, and laying the foundation on which many a beneficent structure was soon to rise." [27] Even more than the intelligentsia, scientists remembered the impression it had made on their youthful minds. Dr. Isaac Ray, before mentioned, in 1879 recalled: "Phrenology was to me, in those days, a revelation of new truths and especially of a philosophy that shed a marvelous light on the whole field of mental science. . . . it gave a turn to my inquiries which I never have ceased to follow, and for which I can never cease to be thankful. No story-book was ever devoured with such abandon of every other thought as Gall's great work 'Sur les Fonctions.' " [28] Even Oliver Wendell Holmes, for all his diatribes against this pseudoscience, recognized its keynote: "Strike out the false pretensions of phrenology; call it anthropology; let it study man the individual in distinction from man the abstraction, the metaphysical or theological lay-figure; and it becomes 'the proper study of mankind,' one of the noblest and most interesting of pursuits." [29]

The central message of phrenology, then, was that man himself could be brought within the purview of science and that mental phenomena could be studied objectively and explained by natural causes; "it is almost correct to say that scientific psychology was born of phrenology, out of wedlock with science." [30] This is what Ray and Holmes saw in these doctrines, a viewpoint which persisted even when the exaggerated claims and unscientific methods of character reading had been exploded. Psychology was removed from the realm of metaphysics and introspection and brought into the sphere of scientific experiment, where it remained even after phrenology itself was discredited. And the idea of this psychology, if not its technical implications, was popularized and taken into common speech; fortified by the new prestige of science, it provided the panacea, the cure-all that the common man sought. Just as do the spate of popular psychology books today, phrenology

27. Theodore Parker, *Works* (Boston, 1907–16), *13*, 309.
28. Capen, *Reminiscences*, p. 139.
29. Holmes, *Writings*, *9*, 245–6.
30. Edwin G. Boring, *A History of Experimental Psychology* (New York, 1929), p. 55.

taught, to quote the title of a plagiarism of *The Constitution of Man*, "The Art of Being Happy."

Thus phrenology was one of the factors which brought science to the American mind and provided a rationalistic explanation of human life. But this it accomplished in a peculiar fashion; with the postulates of science it combined a moralistic deism and a religious teleology—like Silliman's geology, it was a sort of "Christian science." Just as the phrenological *Vestiges of the Natural History of Creation* prepared the way for *On the Origin of the Species* (as Darwin acknowledged in his preface), phrenology provided a way station on the road to a secular view of life. If phrenology in the 1830's and 1840's was a mixture of psychology and philosophy, it was also an unstable compound of science, religion, and morality. In this manner this new science was a precursor of the larger Darwinian movement; years later the same audiences who heard Fowler's lectures and bought Combe's books would be listening to Robert Ingersoll and reading Thomas Huxley.

The decline of phrenology was not rapid, but it may be rapidly described. Like Transcendentalism, it had a one-generation career, and for much the same reasons (or at least with the same symptoms). In the latter 1850's a single reform, abolition, took precedence and subsumed all the rest, and the Gilded Age was a new world. The descendants of the first generation of phrenologists failed to pick up the torch or, for that matter, even to show much interest.

Much of its point had been won, and the movement no longer seemed novel or revolutionary. Its principal credo—that the scientific, experimental approach should be made to operations of the human mind—had suffered scientific euthanasia, incorporated without acknowledgment into contemporary thought, and phrenology was left with the dry husks of its eccentricities—"bumps on the head." In the debate over evolution, over "materialism" versus "spiritualism," phrenology occupied a sort of halfway house and was therefore mute. Herbert Spencer apologized in his autobiography for his early interest in phrenology, and for reasons, interestingly enough, which were precisely contradictory to those used in the first half of the 19th century; in those times, he said, *"Faith was stronger than Scepticism."* [31]

The London Phrenological Society had a disastrous schism in 1843 over the question of embracing a consistently naturalistic philosophy, and as a consequence of the ensuing lack of support four years later the *Phrenological Journal* ceased publication. The only organized channel for intellectual interest in the science was now stilled, and in 1853 when a fifth edition of George Combe's *System of Phrenology* was projected, it was found that there had been no changes or discoveries whatever in the past ten years. In this scientific vacuum the only feature which achieved public notice was the eccentricities of its advocates, unchecked by the contrasting partisans of genuine intellectual stature who had died or lapsed into quiescence. Consequently, by the end of the 19th century the only reason which occurred to Thomas Huxley, when asked why he did not believe in it, was that no other prominent man of science did either. Most of this unfavorable attitude was due to the shift in intellectual fashion and the bleak winds of a new climate of opinion, but there was also the dissemination of new discoveries in neurology; the lecture notes of one postwar student of Dr. Oliver Wendell Holmes read "Annihilation of the phrenologists!" [32] John Morley maintained that at the beginning of the 20th century a belief in phrenology "stamps a man as unscientific."

Such metamorphosis in intellectual trends could have, of course, only a delayed reflex upon practical phrenology. The firm of Fowlers and Wells continued active, optimistic, and prosperous, and the Phrenological Cabinet climbed slowly up Broadway as the center of business shifted on Manhattan. The American Institute of Phrenology was still graduating a class every year in the early 20th century, while the last advertisement of Fowlers and Wells appeared in *Publishers' Weekly* in 1904 and the *American Phrenological Journal* lasted until 1911.

But the firm was compelled to continue without the services of its founders. In 1855 the brothers Fowler sold their interests to

31. Herbert Spencer, *An Autobiography* (2 vols. New York, 1904), *1*, 228.
32. Quoted in Eleanor M. Tilton, *Amiable Autocrat: a Biography of Oliver Wendell Holmes* (New York, 1947), p. 413.

their sister Charlotte and her husband, Samuel R. Wells, and turned their attention exclusively to lecturing and writing, Orson transferring his residence to his home in Fishkill. That building might be taken as a symbol for everything practical phrenology represented: a simple, pseudoscientific, universally efficacious cure-all which was to replace chaos and ugliness with harmony and beauty. The year 1857 saw the eighth (and last) printing of *A Home for All*, the end of the vogue of octagons among Fowler's admirers, the sale of the great home as a boardinghouse, and the onset of a severe depression. The next year its tenants were ravaged by typhoid (his "impermeable" gravel walls had allowed seepage from the cesspool to the well), and "Fowler's Folly" underwent many vicissitudes during the next forty years before being dynamited as a menace to the many sightseers who came to visit it each year. The next "good home" Orson built, at Manchester, Mass., had but one pathetic reminiscence of his brave discoveries—an octagonal dining room. But extensive and lucrative lecture tours continued, as well as his researches into marriage: at the age of seventy-three he took a third wife who bore him three children.

Lorenzo and Lydia Fowler in 1860 made a lecture tour of Great Britain, armed with a letter from their friend Horace Greeley, and this sojourn proved so profitable and pleasant that like their reforming friends, Thomas Low Nichols and Mary Gove Nichols, they settled down in London for the rest of their lives. When Lydia Fowler died in 1879, her daughter Jessie took her mother's place at her father's side and soon was editor of the London *Phrenological Magazine*. In 1896 her father died (at the age of eighty-five) and Jessie returned to America to assume her rightful position in Fowlers and Wells—vice-president of the American Institute of Phrenology, editor-in-chief of the *American Phrenological Journal*, and like all the Fowlers, author of several books on phrenology before her death in 1932. She was the end of a mighty line, the last of the phrenological Fowlers.

APPENDIX

Appendix *

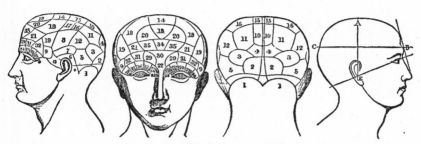

Numbered divisions of the brain

PHRENOLOGY professes to point out a connection between certain
conditions of the brain, and certain manifestations of the mind. It
claims to be a new and complete system of intellectual and moral
philosophy, and also professes to develope new and fundamental
principles of human nature—principles which embrace every thing
pertaining to man as a moral, physical, and intellectual being, and
which are most intimately connected with his happiness and improvement. It rests for support, in part, on the following propositions.

1. The brain is the organ of the mind, or that corporeal instrument which the mind employs in the exercise of thought and feeling. As this proposition is admitted by naturalists, physiologists,
anatomists, metaphysicians, and philosophers generally, I may
take it for granted, and throw the burden of proof on those who
call it in question.

2. The mind is a plurality of innate and independent faculties
—a congregate of distinct and separate powers. This is evident

* An extract from Orson S. Fowler, *Phrenological Chart,* Baltimore, 1836
(italics and capitals have been deleted from the text *passim*).

from the following reasons. 1. It performs different classes of functions, or kinds of operations, such as love, hatred, fear, reason, etc. and, throughout all nature, different kinds of operations are performed by different instruments. The mind, therefore, consists of as many different faculties as it performs different classes of functions. 2. It is often doing several different things at the same time—is often feeling and reasoning, hearing and fearing, seeing and admiring, hating one object and loving another, etc. simultaneously, which could not possibly be done by a single faculty. 3. If the mind were a single faculty, all minds must be exactly alike in their nature, and could differ only in the strength of their qualities and operations, which is not the case. But if different persons possessed the same faculties in different degrees of strength, they must differ accordingly, which is strikingly true. 4. If the mind were a single faculty, it would work just as well in one harness as another—could perform all classes of mental operations with equal facility, which is by no means the case. 5. If the mind were but one faculty, its derangement must equally affect all classes of the mental operations, yet it often affects but a single class. 6. If the mind consisted of several faculties, it could perform not only a greater variety of operations, but also a greater number in a given time, and thus be proportionably the more perfect. 7. Several other reasons might be adduced. 8. Since this proposition is generally admitted, it may with propriety, be assumed. The mind, therefore, consists of innate and independent faculties, several of which can be in simultaneous action.

3. These different faculties are possessed, originally, in different degrees of strength, by the same individual, and also by different individuals. There is a *toto celo* difference between a Shakespeare and a Franklin, a Nero and a Howard, a Raphael and a Washington, a difference which no education could create, nor even essentially modify. Diversity and variety are characteristic no less of the feelings and intellects of men than of their countenances, and that both from the very first dawn of mind, and in opposition to circumstances. The Creator doubtless intended one man for one thing, another for another, and accordingly imparted to them diversity of talents and passions.

4. The brain consists of as many different organs as the mind does of faculties; for, throughout all nature, different classes of functions are always performed by different instruments. There is no example of a single organ performing more than one class of functions. Instead, then, of the whole brain being employed for each class of the mental functions, one portion of it is employed for the exercise of friendship, another, for that of anger, another, for that of reason, etc. The contrary supposition is as absurd, as ridiculous, as contrary to universal analogy, as that the whole body should be employed for seeing, the whole for digestion, etc. In this case also, no two organs could be in simultaneous action, which is contrary to fact.

5. Since one portion of the brain, or one phrenological organ, is allotted exclusively to the exercise of one faculty, and another, to that of another, we may infer, from analogy, the existence of a correspondence between the power of each faculty and the size of its cerebral organ; for, other conditions being equal, *size* is always the measure of power.

6. The exercise of any corporeal organ, of which the brain is one, augments its size. This is an established, and familiar principle of physiology. It follows, then, that if an individual, in the exercise of caution, calls into action one portion of the brain, say that under 12, and in the exercise of benevolence, another portion, say that under 13, he must exercise, and of course increase, that portion under 13, just as much more than that under 12, as he is more benevolent than cautious.

7. The increase of one portion of the brain more than of another, must proportionately elevate that portion of the skull above it; for the shape of the brain determines the shape of the skull, and with few exceptions, corresponds with it. This proposition is established by the great naturalist Cuvier, and susceptible of physical demonstration. If then we can ascertain what portions of the brain are employed by the various faculties, and also how much larger one portion is than another, we can also ascertain even the *minutiae* of a person's character and talents. The thickness of the skull may be determined by its vibrations in speaking, the tones of the voice, etc.

8. The truth of Phrenology is demonstrated chiefly by a world of physical facts. The Phrenological phenomena are uniform, throughout the whole human family—throughout the whole animal kingdom. The whole world is challenged not only to produce a single important exception, but also to examine the facts in the case. This uniformity proves the existence of certain Phrenological *laws* which govern these phenomena. Phrenology, then, is consistent in theory, and susceptible of physical demonstration, by an appeal to nature, and to facts. Let it be judged at this tribunal alone, and stand or fall accordingly. It boldly challenges the most scrutinizing examination. Those who question its truth must disprove the above propositions, and also account for the facts which support Phrenology on other than Phrenological principles. The following are some of the "world of facts" which demonstrate the truth of Phrenology. In the human head there is a large development of the coronal and frontal portions of the head, or of the moral and intellectual organs, while in the animal brain this portion is almost entirely wanting, leaving scarce the least traces of these organs. This corresponds exactly with the mental qualities of the two classes of beings. In the European head there is a much greater endowment of these organs than among any other race. Franklin, Locke, Bacon, Webster, and all powerful and profound thinkers; all deep, original reasoners, without one exception, possess truly immense 34 and 35; men of ordinary minds, a respectable developement of them; the American Indians, Hindoos, Chinese, etc., an inferior developement; the African, still less, and all the lower order of animals, none, or next to none at all. The monkey possesses immense 2 and 22, large 1, 5, 7, etc., but no 33, 34, or 35, which exactly corresponds with the character of that animal. The crow has immense 12, very large 7, large 5, 6, 22, etc.; the fox, cat, and all animals which employ secrecy in catching their prey, possess very large 7, and large 5, 6, and 12; the tiger, lion, leopard, dog, cat, fox, wolf, hawk, eagle, owl, and all those animals of this class, which destroy other animals, and live on their flesh, possess, without one individual exception, immense 6, and large 5, while the sheep, calf, deer, dove, robin, and all those animals which eat no flesh, and are harmless in their nature, have scarce the

least 5 or 6; the dog has very large 29, and accordingly can chase the deer through the forest for successive days, making almost innumerable turnings and windings, and yet know which way home is. These facts might be multiplied ad infinitum, and coincidences added to any extent, between the talents of individuals and their phrenological developements.

Other conditions being equal, the size of the brain is proportionate to the strength of the mind, and the size of each organ, to the strength of the corresponding faculty. Yet very much depends upon the quality and activity of the brain, and this upon the temperament of the subject. When that is very active, a given volume of brain indicates proportionably greater power, so that a small brain may gain in activity what it loses in size. The mental manifestations are affected far more by the temperament, health, habits, etc., than by size. There are four temperaments.

1. The *lymphatic,* or phlegmatic, in which the secreting glands are the most active portion of the system, indicated by soft and abundant flesh, languor of the pulse, and all the vital functions, and aversion to corporeal and mental effort.

2. The *sanguine,* in which the arterial and circulating organs are most active, indicated by light or sandy hair, fair skin, florid countenance, blue eyes, strong and rapid pulse, more ardor and activity than power, and strong animal passions.

3. The *bilious,* in which the muscles predominate in activity, characterized by an athletic form, strong bones and sinews, black hair and eyes, dark skin, strong and steady pulse, hardness, force, and power, but less activity.

4. The *nervous,* in which the brain and nerves are most active, accompanied with the highest degree of activity and excitability of the corporeal and mental powers, vividness and intensity of emotion, rapidity of thought, sprightliness of mind and body, light, fine, and thin hair, a clear and delicate skin, and more activity with less power. These temperaments are generally compounded, the nervo sanguineous giving the highest degree of activity and energy; the nervous bilious, activity and power; the bilious lymphatic, mental and corporeal weakness and indolence, etc. But as these temperaments, and other conditions, except size, are alike in the

same head, it follows that the power and activity of each faculty is proportionate to the size of its organ. Education and circumstances may change the direction of the organs, may greatly modify their manifestation, yet will not materially affect their relative power, unless efforts of the right kind are employed; it may then be done.

The combined action of the organs has also a very great influence on the character, particularly in directing it. The principle is, that the larger organs control and direct the smaller, while the smaller modify the action of the larger. Thus, one having 5 and 6 of a given size, say 12, with 10 very large, will employ his 5 and 6 to avenge personal injuries; promote selfish interests, etc. with 8 very large, in prosecuting money making plans, and defending property; with 13, 14, and 16, very large, in defending suffering innocence, and punishing the aggressor; in maintaining the cause of truth and justice; in driving forward moral and religious, and philanthropic causes, etc. with large intellectual organs, in pursuing intellectual enterprises with vigor; in debating with spirit, etc. with 10 small, and 3 and 13 very large, in defending friends, while he himself endures oppression. As the combinations of these 35 faculties are almost innumerable, especially when taken in connection with the different temperaments, educations, habits, etc. of different persons, there is opened the most expansive field of philosophical research imaginable; a field embracing the whole range of the mental phenomena, and also every thing pertaining to human nature.

Bibliographical Note

THE FOUNDATION of this study has been the files of the *Phreno-logical Journal, and Magazine of Moral Science* (20 vols. Edin-burgh, etc., 1823–47) and the *American Phrenological Journal and Miscellany* (32 vols. Philadelphia and New York, 1838–60), which had not been used by scholars in spite of the fact that their columns provide an epitome of phrenological concepts and a running his-tory of the movement. The New York Public Library has the best collection of printed materials, consisting of about 375 books and pamphlets. The only manuscript materials uncovered which bore directly on the subject were the Fowler-Wells letters, about 175 miscellaneous items in the Collection of Regional History at Cornell University.

The theory and philosophy of phrenology are best studied in Franz Joseph Gall, *On the Origin of the Moral Qualities and In-tellectual Faculties,* trans. Winslow Lewis (6 vols. Boston, 1835) * and in the following works by Johann Gaspar Spurzheim: *The Anatomy of the Brain, with a General View of the Nervous Sys-tem,* revised by Charles H. Stedman, Boston, 1834; *Examination of the Objections Made in Britain against the Doctrines of Gall and Spurzheim,* Boston, 1833; *The Natural Laws of Man,* New York, 1849; *Outlines of Phrenology,* Boston, 1834; *Philosophical Catechism of the Natural Laws of Man,* Boston, 1832; *Phrenology in Connexion with the Study of Physiognomy,* Boston, 1833; *Phrenology; or, the Doctrine of the Mental Phenomena,* Boston,

* Since phrenological books were frequently published in a number of places, at different dates, and with varying paginations, I list only the ed. I used, which is not necessarily the first.

1834; *Sixty Phrenological Specimens, Described by Dr. Spurzheim,* Boston, 1834. George Combe's general works are as follows: *Lectures on Phrenology,* with notes by Andrew Boardman, New York, 1839 (the published lectures delivered on his American tour); *Elements of Phrenology,* Boston, 1834; *Essays on Phrenology,* Philadelphia, 1822; *Lectures on Moral Philosophy,* Boston, 1840; *A System of Phrenology,* Boston, 1834; and most important of all, *The Constitution of Man,* Boston, 1833. Of native American productions I suggest Charles Caldwell, *Elements of Phrenology,* Lexington, 1824; and Amos Dean, *Lectures on Phrenology,* Albany, 1834. Orson Fowler's works are lively and unorthodox: *Phrenology Proved, Illustrated, and Applied,* New York, 1851; *Practical Phrenology,* New York, 1853; *The Practical Phrenologist,* Boston, 1869. He wrote many others, all repetitive of these.

The European background is sketched by Nahum Capen, "Biography of the Author," in Spurzheim, *Phrenology in Connexion with the Study of Physiognomy* (from which comes most of the biographical material of Ch. 2 above), and by Charles Follen, *Funeral Oration . . . of Gaspar Spurzheim,* Boston, 1832. George Combe, *Life and Correspondence of Andrew Combe* (Philadelphia, 1850) is history and autobiography as well. Charles Gibbon, author of *The Life of George Combe* (2 vols. London, 1878) was a friend and sympathizer. Hewett C. Watson, *Statistics of Phrenology* (London, 1836) is a history with figures of the movement in Great Britain, while "Phrenology in France," *Blackwood's Magazine, 82* (1857), 665–74 is a sketchy outline of its Continental career. Of the 20th-century literature see John Knott, "Franz Josef Gall and the Science of Phrenology," *Westminster Review, 166* (1906), 150–63, and Oswei Temkin, "Gall and the Phrenological Movement," *Bulletin of the History of Medicine, 21* (1947), 275–321; the latter is solid.

An outline of early American phrenology is contained in Charles Caldwell, *Autobiography,* Philadelphia, 1855. The Phrenological Society of Washington's *Proceedings . . . Relative to . . . Dr. Thomas Sewall* (Washington, 1826) and *A Report . . . on the Skull of Alexander Tardy* (Washington, 1828) summarize two episodes in that organization's history. George H. Calvert, *Illustrations of Phrenology* (Baltimore, 1832) is one of the first American books on the subject. For Spurzheim's American career, there is, in addition to the Capen and Follen works already cited, Nahum Capen, *Reminiscences of Dr. Spurzheim and George Combe* (New York, 1881) and Park Benjamin, "The Late Dr. Spurzheim," *New England Magazine, 4* (1833), 40–7. Two early magazines were the *Annals of Phrenology* (2 vols. Boston, 1833–36) and the *Phrenological Magazine and New York Literary Review* (1 vol. Utica, 1835). The former was used by John F. Fulton in his "The Early Phrenological Societies and their Journals," *Boston Medical and Surgical Journal, 196* (1927), 398–400. Also on the Boston Phrenological Society is William P. Coues, "The Spurzheim Collection of Phrenological Casts," *op. cit.*, 400–3, and J. Collins Warren, "The Collection of the Boston Phrenological Society—A Retrospect," *Annals of Medical History, 3* (1921), 1–11. An important article is Robert E. Riegel, "Early Phrenology in the United States," *Medical Life, 37* (1930), 361–76, and covering the same ground, his "The Introduction of Phrenology to the United States," *American Historical Review, 39* (1933–34), 73–8. George Combe's American tour is chronicled in his *Notes on the United States . . .* 3 vols. Edinburgh, 1841 or 2 vols. Philadelphia, 1841. Gibbon's biography of Combe has some original material on the United States trip. Roswell W. Haskins has an American survey in *History and Progress of Phrenology*, Buffalo, 1839. The account of two other British phrenologists who wandered around the United States less happily than did Combe are Joshua Toulmin Smith's *Journal in America 1837–1838* (Metuchen, New Jersey, 1925) and Robert H. Collyer's *Lights and Shadows of American Life*, Boston, 1840. The impact of phrenology upon one prominent American reformer is portrayed in Harold Schwartz, "Samuel Gridley Howe as Phrenologist," *American Historical Review, 57* (1951–52), 644–51.

Essential to the history of practical phrenology and of Fowlers and Wells are Nelson Sizer's autobiography, *Forty Years in Phrenology* (New York, 1884) and a retrospective article, "50

Years of Phrenology," *American Phrenological Journal, 80* (1885), 5–31. Carl Carmer has written an amusing and factual article, "That Was New York: the Fowlers, Practical Phrenologists," *New Yorker, 12* (Feb. 13, 1937), 22–7. Some of the numerous books on practical phrenology are: J. G. Buckley, *An Epitome of Phrenology,* Springfield, Ohio, 1848; David P. Butler, *The Phrenological Delineator: a Compendium of Phrenology,* Boston, 1856; John Fletcher, *The Mirror of Nature, Presenting a Brief Sketch of the Science of Phrenology,* Boston, 1842; Orson S. Fowler, *Phrenological Chart,* Baltimore, 1836, and his *Self-instructor in Phrenology and Physiology,* revised ed. New York, 1890; Silas Jones, *Practical Phrenology,* Boston, 1836; J. Kay, *The Phrenologist's Own Book,* Pittsburgh, 1841; A. O'Leary, *Description of Character, as Determined by the Teachings of Physiognomy, Physiology, and Phrenology,* Cincinnati, 1858; C. Townsend, *Improved Phreno-chart,* Ogdensburgh, 1859; and Alexander A. Young, *A Manual of Phrenology,* Philadelphia, 1837.

Popularizations of phrenological concepts published during this period include: Frederick Coombs, *Coombs's Popular Phrenology; Exhibiting the Exact Phrenological Admeasurements of Above Fifty Distinguished and Extraordinary Personages,* Boston, 1841; John Epps, *Horae Phrenologicae,* with notes by Rev. John Pierpont, Boston, 1835; Frank H. Hamilton, *Lectures on Phrenology,* Rochester, 1841; Samuel G. Howe, *The Social Relations of Man,* Boston, 1837; H. T. Judson, *Alphabet of Phrenology; a Short Sketch of That Science for the Use of Beginners,* New York, 1833; R. MacNish, *An Introduction to Phrenology, in the Form of Questions and Answers,* Boston, 1836; Elisha North, *The Pilgrim's Progress in Phrenology,* New London, 1833; and his *Outlines of the Science of Life,* New York, 1829; Thomas W. Olcott, *Address Delivered before the Albany Phrenological Society,* n.d.; Peter Mark Roget, *Outlines of Physiology; with an Appendix on Phrenology,* Philadelphia, 1839; R. C. Rutherford, *A Synopsis of Phrenology,* Conneaut, Ohio, 1848; E. H. Sanford, *An Epitome of Phrenology,* Rochester, 1844; Joshua Toulmin Smith, *Synopsis of Phrenology,* Boston, 1838; L. M. Smith, *The Great American*

*Crisis: or, Cause and Cure of the Rebellion: Embracing Phreno-
logical Characters and Pen-and-Ink Portraits of the President,*
Cincinnati, 1862.

Many anonymous articles on phrenology and reviews of phrenological books were printed in the popular magazines of the day
and may be considered as symptoms of public opinion on that
subject as well as a means of shaping that opinion: "A Familiar
Essay on Phrenology," *American Monthly Magazine,* 2 (1838),
455–7; "Combe on The Constitution of Man," *American Monthly
Review, 3* (1833), 417–23; "Phrenology," *American Quarterly Review, 20* (1836), 366–94; "Gall and Spurzheim's System of Phrenology," *Analectic Magazine, 6* (1815), 63–9; "Phrenology," *Biblical Repertory and Princeton Review, 10* (1838), 279–320; "Phrenology," *op. cit., 21* (1849), 298–300; "Dr. Spurzheim's Works,"
Boston Literary Magazine, 1 (1833), 434–40; "Pretensions of
Phrenology," *Boston Quarterly Review,* 2 (1839), 205–29; "The
Constitution of Man Considered in Relation to External Objects,"
Christian Examiner, 12 (1832), 385–404; "Moral Aspects of Phrenology," *op. cit., 16* (1834), 221–48; "Physiology," *Family Magazine, 1* (1833–34), 130–1; "Phrenology," *op. cit.,* p. 142; "Literary
Notices," *Knickerbocker, 1* (1833), 315–16; *ibid., 4* (1834), 77–8;
ibid., 8 (1836), 615–17; "A Few Thoughts on Phrenology," *op. cit.,
10* (1837), 417–22; "Phrenology Made Easy," *op. cit., 11* (1838),
523–7; "Hints about Phrenology," *Ladies' Magazine, 6* (1833),
24–7, 135–8, 174–5, 225–6, 277–80, 368, 426–7, 497–505; "Notices,"
Ladies' Repository, 7 (1847), 29–31; "Literary Notices," *New England Magazine, 4* (1833), 334–5; *ibid., 5* (1833), 78–80; "Phrenology
Vindicated," *op. cit., 7* (1834), 14–19, 433–4; "Phrenology and Free
Will," *op. cit., 8,* 115–18; "Answer to the Article on Phrenology, in
the Christian Examiner," *op. cit.,* 182–93; "Literary Notices," *New
York Mirror, 14* (1836–37), 247; "Combe's Moral Philosophy,"
New York Review, 1 (1837), 218–25; "Phrenology," *North American Review, 37* (1833), 59–83; "Combe's Phrenological Visit,"
op. cit., 53 (1841), 534–6; "Literary Notices," *Portfolio, 8* (1819),
516–18; "On Cranioscopy," *op. cit., 13* (1822), 353–72; "Phrenological Examinations," *Southern Literary Messenger, 1* (1834–35),

188   PHRENOLOGY, FAD AND SCIENCE

204–5; "Phrenology," *op. cit.*, *2* (1836), 286; "Phrenology Examined," *op. cit.*, *12* (1846), 267–77; "Gall on the Functions of the Brain," *Southern Review*, *1* (1828), 134–59; "Mental Development," *op. cit.*, *6* (1830), 265–83; "Phrenology," *Western Monthly Magazine*, *1* (1833), 241–7; "Combe's Constitution of Man," *Yale Literary Magazine*, *11* (1845–46), 306–10.

Signed articles in the popular press include George Combe's American lectures, which were reprinted serially in the *New Yorker*, 7 (1839), 65–7, 81–4, 97–9, 113–15, 129–31, 145–7, 161–4, 177–9, 193–5, 209–11, 225–7, 241–3, 257–60, 273–6, 289–91, 305–7, and in the *Southern Literary Messenger*, 5 (1838), 393–7, 459–64, 567–70, 602–5, 667–70, 766–70, 810–13. For articles whose authors can be identified see Caleb Cushing, "Delusions of Science," *National Magazine and Republican*, *1* (1839), 147–62, 235–59; Park Benjamin, "The Late Dr. Spurzheim," *New England Magazine*, *4* (1833), 40–7, and his "Phrenology," *op. cit.*, *6* (1834), 467–79; Russell Jarvis, "On the Humbug of Phrenology," *Burton's Gentleman's Magazine*, 7 (1840), 62–9; Samuel Gridley Howe, "The Heads of our Great Men," 5 (1841), 354–64, and his "Phrenology," *North American Review*, 56 (1843), 171–91; E. P. Hurlbut, "On Rights and Government," *United States Magazine and Democratic Review*, *9* (1841), 459–76, 568–83; Frederick H. Hedge, "Pretensions of Phrenology Examined," *Christian Examiner*, *17* (1835), 249–69; Benjamin Silliman, "Obituary Notice of Dr. Gaspar Spurzheim," *American Journal of Science*, *33* (1833), 356–70.

The application of phrenology to education may be studied in Johann Gaspar Spurzheim, *A View of the Elementary Principles of Education*, Boston, 1833; George Combe, *Education, Its Principles and Practices*, London, 1879; Andrew Combe, *A Treatise on the Physiological and Moral Management of Infancy*, Boston, 1846; Orson S. Fowler, *Education and Self-improvement*, New York, 1883; his *Phrenology and Physiology Explained and Applied to Education and Self-improvement*, New York, 1843; his *Fowler on Memory: or, Phrenology Applied to the Cultivation of Memory: the Intellectual Education of Children, and the Strengthening and Expanding of the Intellectual Powers*, New York and

Philadelphia, 1842; Mrs. Lorenzo N. Fowler, *Familiar Lessons on Phrenology, Designed for the Use of Children and Youth in Schools and Families,* New York, 1848; William L. Crandal, *Three Hours School a Day: a Talk with Parents,* Albany, 1854; Nelson Sizer, *How to Teach according to Temperament and Mental Development; or Phrenology in the School-room and the Family,* New York, 1877; Joseph A. Warne, *Phrenology in the Family, the Utility of Phrenology in Early Domestic Education,* Philadelphia, 1839; James Simpson, *Necessity of Popular Education as a National Object; with Hints on the Treatment of Criminals, and Observations on Homicidal Insanity,* Boston, 1834; "Review of Spurzheim on Education," *American Annals of Education, 3* (1833), 123–8; "Combe's Lectures on Popular Education," *op. cit., 4* (1834), 395–9; "Connection of the Mind and the Brain," *op. cit., 5* (1835), 490–2; "Combe on the Constitution of Man," *American Journal of Education, 4* (1829), 289–300; "Constitution of Man," *op. cit.,* 506–31; "Remarks on the Science of Phrenology," *op. cit.,* 541–3; and Timothy Flint, "Thoughts on the Philosophy of Education," *Western Monthly Review, 3* (1829–30), 393–402, 449–59.

Phrenology is related to penology in the following works: Charles Caldwell, *New Views of Penitentiary Discipline,* Lexington, Ky., 1827; George Combe, *Remarks on the Principles of Criminal Legislation,* London, 1854; James Simpson, *Necessity of Popular Education as a National Object; with Hints on the Treatment of Criminals, and Observations on Homicidal Insanity,* Boston, 1834; Timothy Flint, "Penitentiary Discipline," *Western Monthly Review, 3* (1829–30), 50–6; Marmaduke B. Sampson, *Rationale of Crime and Its Appropriate Treatment,* New York, 1846; Samuel Gridley Howe, *Essay on the Separate and Congregate Systems of Prison Discipline,* Boston, 1846.

The treatment of insanity by means of phrenology is explained in Johann Gaspar Spurzheim, *Observations on the Deranged Manifestations of the Mind, or Insanity,* with appendix by Amariah Brigham, Boston, 1833; Andrew Combe, *Observations on Mental Derangement: Being an Application of the Principles of Phrenology to the Elucidation of the Causes, Symptoms, Nature, and*

Treatment of Insanity, with notes and bibliography by "an American physician," Boston, 1834; Amariah Brigham, *An Inquiry concerning the Diseases and Functions of the Brain, the Spinal Cord, and the Nerves,* New York, 1840; Isaac Ray, *A Treatise on the Medical Jurisprudence of Insanity,* Boston, 1838; his *Mental Hygiene,* Boston, 1863; his *Education in Its Relation to the Physical Health of the Brain,* Boston, 1850; H. A. Buttolph, "The Relation between Phrenology and Insanity," *American Journal of Insanity, 6* (1849), 49–59, 127–36; N. S. Davis, "Importance of a Correct Physiology of the Brain," *op. cit., 1* (1844–45), 235–43; "Definition of Insanity—Nature of the Disease," *op. cit.,* pp. 97–116.

The importance of phrenology for the medical profession as a whole is indicated by Franz Joseph Gall, *On the Origin of the Moral Qualities and Intellectual Faculties,* trans. Winslow Lewis, 6 vols. Boston, 1835; Johann Gaspar Spurzheim, *The Anatomy of the Brain, with a General View of the Nervous System,* revised by Charles H. Stedman, Boston, 1834; John W. Draper, *Human Physiology,* New York, 1858; Robley Dunglison, *Human Physiology,* 2 vols. Philadelphia, 1841; John Elliotson, *Physiology,* London, 1840; Samuel Jackson, *The Principles of Medicine,* Philadelphia, 1832; William S. Kirkes and James Paget, *Manual of Physiology,* Philadelphia, 1849; John Mackintosh, *Principles of Pathology and Practice of Medicine,* with notes and additions by Samuel G. Morton, Philadelphia, 1844; Daniel Noble, *The Brain and Its Physiology,* London, 1846. Some unsigned articles in the medical press are as follows: "Lectures on Phrenology," *Boston Medical and Surgical Journal, 7* (1832), 162; "Death of Dr. Spurzheim," *op. cit.,* 225–7; "Professor Follen's Funeral Oration," *op. cit.,* 319–24; "Spurzheim on Phrenology," *American Journal of the Medical Sciences, 12* (1833), 473–7; "Phrenology," *Eclectic Journal of Medicine, 1* (1836–37), 126–35; "Andrew Combe, Remarks on Tiedeman's Comparison of the Negro Brain and Intellect with Those of the European," *op. cit., 2* (1837–38), 325–8; "Phrenology in the Family," *op. cit., 3* (1838–39), 310–11; "John Bell on Phrenology," *Philadelphia Journal of the Medical and*

Physical Sciences, 4 (1822), 72–113; "Combe on Phrenology," *op. cit., 5* (1822), 398–424; "B. H. Coates on Comparative Phrenology," *op. cit., 7* (1823), 58–80; "Phrenology," *op. cit., 8* (1824), 171–214. The importance of phrenology for the study of skulls is explained in Samuel G. Morton, *Crania Americana,* with appendix by George Combe, Philadelphia, 1839; Thomas Sewall's medical indictment of phrenology is entitled *An Examination of Phrenology,* Boston, 1839; Pierre Flourens' was translated into English by Charles D. Meigs under the title *Phrenology Examined,* Philadelphia, 1846.

For the insights of phrenology into the problem of physical health see Charles Caldwell, *Thoughts on Physical Education,* Boston, 1834; Andrew Combe, *The Principles of Physiology Applied to the Preservation of Health, and to the Improvement of Physical and Mental Education,* New York, 1834; Amariah Brigham, *Remarks on the Influence of Religion and Physical Welfare of Mankind,* Boston, 1833; Orson S. Fowler, *Physiology Animal and Mental,* New York, 1847; Mrs. Lorenzo N. Fowler, *Familiar Lessons on Physiology, Designed for the Use of Children and Youth in Schools and Families,* New York, 1848. A special branch of health is outlined by Orson S. Fowler in *Phrenology vs. Intemperance,* New York, 1841. On "domestic economy" there is Orson S. Fowler, *Fowler on Matrimony,* New York, 1841; his *Matrimony, as Taught by Phrenology and Physiology,* New York, 1859; his *Hereditary Descent: Its Laws and Facts Applied to Human Improvement,* New York, 1843; his *Sexual Science,* New York, 1870; Lorenzo N. Fowler, *The Principles of Phrenology and Physiology Applied to Man's Social Relations; together with an Analysis of the Domestic Feelings,* New York, 1842; his *Marriage: Its History and Ceremonies,* New York, 1847; Nelson Sizer, *Thoughts on Domestic Life: or, Marriage Vindicated and Free Love Exposed,* New York, 1848; his *Cupid's Eyes Opened and Mirror of Matrimony,* Hartford, 1848. For the water cure see Thomas Low Nichols, *Introduction to the Water-cure* (New York, 1840) and the files of *The Water Cure Journal,* 33 vols. New York, 1845–61.

There are several books on mesmerism and its alliance with phrenology: Charles Poyen Saint Sauveur, *Progress of Animal Magnetism in New England,* Boston, 1837; Charles Caldwell, *Facts on Mesmerism and Thoughts on its Causes and Uses,* Louisville, 1842; Charles P. Johnson, *Treatise on Animal Magnetism,* New York, 1842; William Lang, *Mesmerism: Its History, Phenomena, and Practice,* Edinburgh, 1843; and an anonymous article, "Animal Magnetism," *Eclectic Journal of Medicine,* 2 (1837–38), 22–36. See also the files of the *New York Magnet* (3 vols. New York, 1842–44) and the *Journal of the Phreno-Magnetic Society of Cincinnati,* 1 vol. Cincinnati, 1842.

Some of the works of deviators from conventional phrenology are J. Stanley Grimes, *A New System of Phrenology,* Buffalo, 1839; his *Phreno-geology,* Boston, 1851; his *Etherology: or, the Philosophy of Mesmerism and Phrenology,* New York, 1845; on Grimes himself there is E. N. Horsford, *Report on the Phrenological Classification of J. Stanley Grimes,* Albany, 1840. Another deviator was Joseph Rodes Buchanan, *Outlines of Lectures on the Neurological System of Anthropology, as Discovered, Demonstrated and Taught in 1841 and 1842,* Cincinnati, 1854; his *Therapeutic Sarcognomy,* Boston, 1884; his *Manual of Psychometry: the Dawn of a New Civilization,* Boston, 1885; his *Primitive Christianity,* San Jose, Cal., 1898. For Buchanan see Hugh M. Ayer, "Joseph Rodes Buchanan," unpublished M.A. thesis, Indiana University, 1949. Others were John S. Hittell, *A New System of Phrenology* (New York, 1857) and Joachim D. L. Zender, *Andronomy, or Magneto-physiognomico-craniology,* New York, 1859.

The application of phrenology to art is outlined in George Combe, *Phrenology Applied to Painting and Sculpture* (London, 1855) and in Edward Hungerford's scholarly "Poe and Phrenology," *American Literature,* 2 (1930–31), 209–31, and his "Walt Whitman and His Chart of Bumps," *op. cit.,* 350–84. Herbert R. Brown, *The Sentimental Novel in America, 1789–1860* (Durham, N.C., 1940) cites several examples of phrenology in literature. Orson Fowler's theories of architecture are illustrated in his *A Home for All, or The Gravel Wall and Octagon Mode of Building* (New York, 1851), explained in Walter Creese's excellent "Orson Squire

Fowler and the Domestic Octagon," *Art Bulletin, 28* (1946), 89–102.

The following works assert that phrenology is subversive of organized Christianity: Nathan L. Rice, *Phrenology Examined, and Shown to Be Inconsistent with the Principles of Physiology, Mental and Moral Science, and the Doctrines of Christianity. Also an Examination of the Claims of Mesmerism,* New York and Cincinnati, 1849; Walter Edgerton, *A Brief Review of Certain Phrenological Works of O. S. Fowler,* Newport, Iowa, 1848; John Manesca, *Strictures on Phrenology,* New York, 1832; John Augustine Smith, *Select Discourses on the Functions of the Nervous System, in Opposition to Phrenology, Materialism, and Atheism,* New York, 1840; John Byrne, *Anti-phrenology, or, A Chapter on Humbug,* Washington, 1843; David M. Reese, *The Humbugs of New York,* New York, 1838. These books deny that there is any conflict between phrenology and the true spirit of Christianity: John Epps, *Internal Evidences of Christianity, Deduced from Phrenology,* with preface and notes by Joseph A. Warne, Boston, 1837; Joseph A. Warne, *On the Harmony between the Scriptures and Phrenology,* Boston, 1837; John Pierpont, *Phrenology and the Scriptures,* New York, 1850; William Ingalls, *A Lecture on the Subject of Phrenology Not Opposed to the Principles of Religion,* Boston, 1839; Edward Hitchcock, *Religious Truth, Illustrated from Science, in Addresses and Sermons on Special Occasions,* Boston, 1857; John C. Tomlinson, "The Science of Phrenology Consistent with the Doctrine of Christianity," *Pamphleteer, 26* (1826), 415–25. Orson S. Fowler, *The Christian Phrenologist,* Cazenovia, New York, 1843; his *Religion Natural and Revealed,* New York, 1843. Finally, these works admit that a certain amount of conflict exists but are inclined to take the side of phrenology: Charles Caldwell, *Thoughts on the True Connexion of Phrenology and Religion,* Lexington, Kentucky, 1839; Amariah Brigham, *Observations on the Influence of Religion on the Physical Welfare of Mankind,* Boston, 1835; Edgar C. Beall, *The Brain and the Bible; or, the Conflict between Mental Science and Theology,* with preface by Robert G. Ingersoll, Cincinnati, 1882; and the files of the *Zoist,* 13 vols. London, 1843–56.

There are a number of lively social histories about the matrix of pre-Civil War reforms: Alice Felt Tyler, *Freedom's Ferment*, Minneapolis, 1944; Carl R. Fish, *The Rise of the Common Man, 1830–1850*, New York, 1927; E. Douglas Branch, *The Sentimental Years, 1836–1860*, New York, 1934; Robert E. Riegel, *Young America, 1830–1840*, Norman, Oklahoma, 1949; Gilbert Seldes, *The Stammering Century*, New York, 1927; Grace Adams and Edward Hutter, *The Mad Forties*, New York, 1942. The latter four give passing mention to phrenology, although the last is not very reliable. Three books are helpful for medical background: Madge E. Pickard and R. Carlyle Buley, *The Midwest Pioneer: His Ills, Cures, and Doctors*, New York, 1946; Henry B. Shafer, *The American Medical Profession, 1783 to 1850*, New York, 1936; William F. Norwood, *Medical Education in the United States before the Civil War*, Philadelphia, 1944. The standard work on penology is Blake McKelvey, *American Prisons*, Chicago, 1936; on insane asylums, Albert Deutsch, *The Mentally Ill in America*, Garden City, N.Y., 1937; on journalism, Frank Luther Mott, *A History of American Magazines, 1741–1850*, New York, 1930. Burke A. Hinsdale, *Horace Mann and the Common School Revival in the United States* (New York, 1898, 1937) is much more than a biography. Richard H. Shryock, "Sylvester Graham and the Popular Health Movement, 1830–1870," *Mississippi Valley Historical Review, 18* (1931–32), 172–83, is an important article. Merle Curti, *The Growth of American Thought* (New York, 1943) has some brief but provocative suggestions about the role of phrenology.

Two other studies devoted to the importation of European social philosophies conditioned my thinking: Richard Hofstadter, *Social Darwinism in American Thought, 1860–1915* (Philadelphia, 1944) and Frederick J. Hoffman, *Freudianism and the Literary Mind*, Baton Rouge, La., 1945. On the theory of intellectual history, Dixon Ryan Fox, *Ideas in Motion* (New York, 1935) and Franklin L. Baumer, "Intellectual History and Its Problems," *Journal of Modern History, 21* (1949), 191–203, offered thoughtful leads. Finally, there is Ralph L. Gabriel, *The Course of American Democratic Thought*, New York, 1940.

Index